Hillstrom's 2011 Almanac

Restoring Sanity To Marketing, Analytics, and Leadership With 365 Facts,
Opinions, And Ideas To Immediately Improve Business Results

Kevin Hillstrom

Acknowledgements

I would like to thank those who follow me on Twitter, and read my blog. Your recommendations to tweet less and to better document my concepts and ideas led to the creation of this book!

13 Digit ISBN: 978-1-4563-4013-1

Published in the United States of America by Kevin Hillstrom

To order books:
http://amazon.com

Manufactured in the United States of America
First Edition

Cover Design: Kevin Hillstrom and Createspace.com
Cover Art: Kevin Hillstrom and http://istockphoto.com

Table of Contents

Biography

Kevin Hillstrom is a database marketing veteran with more than twenty years of experience analyzing customer behavior at many of America's greatest multichannel retailers.

Kevin began his professional career in 1998 as a Statistical Analyst at the Garst Seed Company, analyzing corn and sorghum trials.

In 1990, Kevin became a Statistical Analyst at Lands' End. It was at Lands' End where Kevin learned many of the tricks and techniques required to effectively model customer behavior. Kevin worked with a very bright direct marketing team, developing experiments that explained how customers interacted with different catalog titles over time, learning all about the ways that cannibalization of marketing activities erode company profitability. Kevin ended his tenure at Lands' End in late 1995, as Manager of Analytical Services.

In 1995, Kevin became Manager of Analytical Services at Eddie Bauer. Working with an integrated database (retail, catalog, online transactions), Kevin was able to demonstrate how customer behavior changed when new stores were opened in new markets, and how customer behavior changed when new stores were opened in existing markets. As Director of Circulation, Kevin partnered with a seasoned team of Executives to deliver the most profit ever generated by the direct-to-consumer division (catalog + internet), by reducing promotions (free shipping, % off offers), reducing catalog advertising to retail and online customers, and by using advanced statistical models to target customers with appropriate direct mail offerings. It was at Eddie Bauer that Kevin developed the methodologies that would ultimately become the foundation of "Multichannel Forensics".

Following a nine month stint as a Sr. Consultant at Avenue A, Kevin became Vice President of Direct Marketing at Nordstrom. The Executive team at Nordstrom Direct was charged with turning around a business that generated more than $300,000,000 in annual sales, but was losing more than $30,000,000 in profit each year. Within just two years, Kevin and his Executive team partners were able to re-calibrate catalog contact strategies and online marketing activities, bringing the business back to break-even.

In 2003, Kevin became Vice President of Database Marketing, working in the corporate office. Kevin's team was asked to integrate outbound customer marketing strategies (direct mail, catalogs, e-mail marketing), using an integrated transactional database. In 2004, Kevin was part of a team that decided to eliminate traditional catalog marketing, a decision that was widely criticized by purveyors of existing marketing best practices. In fact, Kevin was skeptical, too. However, within twelve months of eliminating a traditional catalog marketing program, retail comp store sales continued to increase, and without the support of catalog marketing, online sales actually increased at a rapid rate. It was at Nordstrom that the final touches were put on the "Multichannel Forensics" framework that accurately suggested that retail and online channels did not need catalog mailings to support sales growth.

In March 2007, Kevin left Nordstrom to begin his own consulting practice, called "MineThatData". Kevin utilizes his Multichannel Forensics framework to help marketers understand how customers interact with products, brands, and channels. Kevin's clients include online pure-plays, thirty million dollar catalog brands, billion dollar retail multichannel brands, and international direct marketers.

Following the collapse of the economy in 2007-2008, CEOs began asking different questions, questions that focused on the long-term sales trajectory of online advertising micro-channels. Kevin expanded his Multichannel Forensics framework, resulting in what are called "Online Marketing Simulations", tools that allows CEOs, CMOs, Online Marketers, and Web Analysts to understand how online and offline customers are likely to evolve and change in the future. This information allows the online marketer to identify the "Most Valuable Path", or "MVP", the path that maps how first time buyers become loyal customers. Armed with this information, investments in keyword campaigns, affiliate marketing, and e-mail marketing change, resulting in an improved and more profitable future.

And in 2010, CEOs asked a new set of questions, questions about customer behavior. Kevin created a new segmentation methodology called "Digital Profiles", designed to combine recency, frequency, and monetary information with the channels a customer purchases from, and the merchandise divisions a customer prefers, yielding sixteen actionable segments that can be used for targeting purposes, e-mail marketing strategy, catalog circulation strategy, online targeting, and general business intelligence.

Kevin also hosts the highly popular database marketing blog, called "The MineThatData Blog", where Kevin discusses online marketing, direct marketing, database marketing, and multichannel marketing topics on a frequent basis. You can also follow Kevin on Twitter!

Contact Information:

Kevin Hillstrom
E-Mail: kevinh@minethatdata.com
Website: http://minethatdata.com
Blog: http://blog.minethatdata.com
Twitter: http://twitter.com/minethatdata

Consulting Services

Kevin provides consulting services for leading online marketers and multichannel retailers. Given his experience at leading multichannel retailers like Nordstrom, Eddie Bauer, Lands' End, and more than four-dozen consultations with direct marketers and retailers, Kevin brings more than two decades of unique executive and analytical experience to his projects.

There are many popular projects that Kevin performs for CEOs and CMOs.

- Digital Profiles, segmentation projects resulting in sixteen actionable customer personas based on recency, frequency, monetary value, channel preference, merchandise preference, social media activity, and mobile channel activity. The segments are used for a variety of customer targeting and business intelligence initiatives.

- Multichannel Forensics and Online Marketing Simulation Projects, designed to determine which customers no longer need to receive catalog mailings, and outline which customers should receive a mix of e-mail marketing and catalog marketing. A typical Multichannel Forensics Project for a $75,000,000 brand results in about $250,000 to $750,000 of annual profit opportunity, well worth the average cost of a Multichannel Forensics project. A typical Multichannel Forensics or Online Marketing Simulation project takes four weeks to complete, and costs between $10,000 and $40,000, depending upon how many twelve-month buyers your business manages.

- Price Elasticity Projects, where we determine how many units of an item will sell, given different pricing strategies. You will learn which price generates the most gross margin dollars for a given item, and you will receive a spreadsheet that allows you to play with different scenarios.

- Database Marketing Audits, designed to help the CEO/CMO understand how your business stacks up against competing organizations. The typical two-day audit results in a roadmap for success, outlining database strategies and marketing strategies and staffing strategies that yield profitable outcomes.

Contact me (kevinh@minethatdata.com) for project details.

Introduction

It was late September, 2010.

At the time, about 2,100 folks followed me on Twitter.

I was writing a series of tweets called "For / Against". Basically, I would say I was against topic, something that I call "marketing slush". Here's an example of something I am against:

- "Three quick and easy ways to grow your online business during the Holiday season."

Believe me, if there were three quick and easy ways to grow your business during the Holiday season, everybody would be doing it, or the person who possessed said knowledge would sell the ideas for millions of dollars.

That's an example of something that I am against.

I'm for hard work. I don't think there are many shortcuts. There's genius, the kind of genius you see when a merchant accurately identifies a trend, takes a risk on product months in advance, and then markets it to a loyal customer base who trusts her instincts. I'm for that!

So I was sharing these "For / Against" tweets with the audience. After sharing about ten of these "For / Against" tweets, a funny thing happened. Those who followed me rebelled!

- "Stop spamming us with your goofy thoughts. If I want your opinion, I'll ask for it."
- "Slow down how many tweets you publish each day. Nobody wants this much information!"
- "You are interrupting my Twitter stream. I want to see a diversity of thought, not just your thoughts."
- "Twitter is an inappropriate place to share this kind of information, you should share it on your blog."
- "You obviously don't know anything about social media, or you wouldn't pummel us like this. The community dictates what is right and wrong."
- "You shouldn't share this information on your blog because that's not the right place for it, you should share it in a book."

Within a week, five percent of those who followed me on Twitter abandoned my content.

One woman told me that she'd rather read drivel than read actionable and frequently distributed facts. I asked this individual if she really valued infrequent drivel over a stream of actionable facts. This was her response:

- "I think it is better if you just share one fact a day. That way, people can digest your content without being overwhelmed."
- "And if your content is documented somewhere, people could go back and re-read it so that it isn't lost in the stream."

Hmmmm.

This book is a response to my experiences writing a marketing/analytics blog for the past five years, coupled with my experiences interacting with individuals on Twitter.

Each day, I'm going to offer you a fact or an opinion. Some days, the content is as long as a tweet (140 characters). Some days, you're going to read an essay. On other days, you'll be given actionable tools to immediately grow and improve your business, based on the analytical work I've done for more than fifty companies over the past three years , based on two decades of marketing/analytics work at Nordstrom, Eddie Bauer, and Lands' End.

There won't be a rhyme or reason to the content. Sometimes topics will have a flow to them. I may spend a week, or even a month, talking about one specific topic. Then I might spend two weeks talking about unrelated and random topics. That's the nature of life, and Twitter for that matter!

Don't expect this book to be grammatically perfect. I'm self-publishing this, as a response to a marketing/analytics community that wanted the content in a different format. The goal is to get your actionable content that improves business performance, I'm sure you value actionable content more than anything else.

Expect this book to sometimes ruffle feathers. We're drowning in an endless vat of marketing slush. The marketing/analytics world is now consumed by extreme agendas and hype. One expert tells us we'll be out of business if we keep using direct mail and fail to adapt to a mobile marketing world. Another marketing expert tells us we'll be out of business if we don't use print to drive customers to mobile marketing. We're being pummeled by a vendor community that is trying to sell thought leadership, thought leadership that then sells consulting projects, software, or hardware. So much of what we read represents extreme viewpoints. So little of what we read represents what average people use to make incremental gains in real businesses. This isn't a criticism of the vendor community. The overwhelming vast majority of folks working in the vendor community are trying to do good. Some of the publicly distributed content from the vendor community, however, represents extreme viewpoints. That's what I am going to focus on.

I'm going to use a style of communication preferred by my blog and Twitter followers to outline actionable strategies that you can immediately use to generate incremental profit. I'm going to point out some of the marketing slush we have to navigate each and every day. I hope to encourage you to be an "independent thought leader".

This is important, folks. I recently spoke with a marketing executive at a major brand that almost all of us have heard about. This business leader offered a half-dozen industry buzzwords in a half-hour discussion. This business leader had no facts to back up the theory behind the industry buzzwords, instead, the leader trusted the vendor community promoting the buzzwords.

I run into this over and over again. The vendor community isn't evil by any stretch of the imagination. Unfortunately, the vendor community (and consultants like me) promotes extreme positions using metrics from $1,699 research reports (metrics acquired from 883 customers) to frighten marketers and analytics experts into buying products and services that make the vendor community additional profit. Without valid data to refute the information being shared, marketers and analytics experts begin to adopt extreme positions and research report metrics as fact, building a house of cards on top of marketing slush.

My job is to offer you facts and opinions that increase your business. More than anything, I want for you to be an "independent thought leader", cobbling together reasonable facts backed by real customer data to do what is right for your customers and your business. You need for your business to be more profitable. You don't need to buy products and services that may or may not grow your business, but will surely result in an increase in profit for the company you buy the products and services from!

Please give this format a try. I'm only offering one tidbit a day, that's not too much to handle, is it? Maintain your position as an "independent thought leader" while reading the content. Apply the content to your business, and see if it works. What I recommend won't work for every business, I'll be the first to admit that. But if you can shovel the marketing slush from your driveway, you may find that a handful of the tidbits I'm going to share will apply to your business. Combine what I share, based on research across fifty retail, online, and catalog brands, with your own business brilliance.

Let me know what you think, I'm open to positive and negative feedback. E-mail me your thoughts (kevinh@minethatdata.com) or tweet your responses to @minethatdata.

Hillstrom's 2011 Almanac

January 1

It is the first day of a new year. For many folks, January 1 is a day of excitement, of rebirth. It can be hard to predict how a new year will turn out. After all, it is the middle of Winter, with Spring many months away.

And yet, Spring will come. When it comes, you want to be ready for Spring. If you are an outdoor enthusiast, you'll be fully prepared for that first glorious seventy degree afternoon, won't you? You'll spend the next three months preparing for a day that you know will come, but you cannot pinpoint the exact day when beautiful weather will arrive.

Marketing and analytics aren't any different, really. Many companies begin their fiscal year on or around January 1. Some employees receive a new set of goals and objectives, a set of initiatives that define the work the employee will do in the upcoming year.

Why not spend time today crafting a new strategy for the upcoming year?

Do something different. Create an initiative for yourself, and don't tell anybody. Don't ask for permission, because if you ask for permission, somebody is going to tell you "no".

Set out to learn something new this year. Take it upon yourself to create a new product, to learn how to use a new piece of software, to create a new marketing strategy to acquire new customers. Craft a timeline that you'll chart your progress against.

And then, sometime this Spring, on that first seventy degree day, spring your new concept, strategy, or product upon your company, or introduce it to your customer base.

January 2

Some folks might head to the mall on a Sunday in January. They'll load their cars with unwanted Christmas gifts, looking to return the items for cash.

Marketers and analytics experts have an opportunity, an opportunity to analyze customers who return merchandise.

There is a huge difference in customer value among various customers. Some customers pay full price and keep their merchandise. Some customers buy merchandise on sale and return their merchandise. Other customers return merchandise that friends or family purchased for them.

Make a resolution to analyze customers who return merchandise. Identify customers who purchase multiple times, and return more than half of their merchandise. This won't be a large audience, but it is an audience worth eliminating marketing activities to, as there is no reason to lose money on purpose. Let this audience shop, but curtail marketing activities to this audience.

January 3

The first Monday of the new work year. Your co-workers will stagger into the office. Some of your co-workers haven't been at work in two weeks. They will be greeted with 274 e-mail messages, many of which are no longer relevant.

Today, spend some time analyzing your e-mail marketing campaigns from the Holiday season, and identify the campaigns that were not relevant to your customer audience!

January 4

This is the time of year that customers redeem gift cards. Gift card customers fall into two camps, those who purchase gift cards for others, and those who redeem gift cards.

Without a doubt, customers in each camp should be segmented differently. So often, the gift card purchaser or redeemer has a different level of future value than the average customer. Use your analytics tools to carefully measure how these customers perform in the days after buying a gift card, or in the days after redeeming a gift card. Overlay prior purchase information against the gift card buyer/redeemer, and profile these customers. Measure how many new customers you acquire among those who redeem gift cards.

Paint a picture of the gift card buyer/redeemer, and share that picture with your management team. Gift card buyer/redeemers are seldom average, they are often great customers, or are infrequent buyers. Segment these customers properly!

January 5

A lot of folks want to sell you stuff. And they sell you stuff in very sneaky ways. Take trade journals and conference publications, for instance. How often have you read a headline like this:

"Three Quick Tips To Mobile Marketing Success"

Or this:

"Four Ways That Social Media Will Revolutionize Customer Engagement"

Oh boy.

With every marketing article you read in 2011, ask yourself a simple question:

>   Question: What is the author selling?

Too often, the author is giving us a series of easy tips or ideas that barely benefit us, but clearly benefit the author. Our job in 2011 is to ferret out the truth from the truthiness. Question everything you read. Look for articles that refer to "profit", articles that clearly demonstrate an increase in profit because of the strategy outlined in the article. Avoid articles that cloak benefits in terms like "engagement" or "conversations". Be wary of any author that tells you that you will be out of business in 2013 if you don't immediately adopt the strategy the author recommends. Stay away from articles that use phrases like *"... in these challenging economic times, savvy marketers are discovering the power of ..."*

Ferret out truth from all of the truthiness you'll read in 2011.

January 6

Ask your boss to send you to one professional development activity in 2011. Ask now, so that your request is tallied in your company budget for the upcoming fiscal year.

January 7

Find one company in your industry who you do not compete with, but you admire from afar. Use LinkedIn to find your peer at that company. Offer your peer an opportunity for a "knowledge exchange". This is a one-day or two-day meeting that you schedule at the site of the company you wish to learn about. During this one or two day session, teams from each company share how they execute marketing and analytics, sharing "best practices" with each other.

Too often, we view everything we do as "proprietary".

Too often, we fail to see how our efforts could be complemented with efforts from others at non-competing brands, yielding new and actionable strategies.

Take advantage of peers at non-competing brands, offering a collaborative and mutually beneficial relationship.

January 8

It's a Saturday. You should be spending time with your family, but instead, you find yourself checking e-mail on your mobile phone.

If you are going to spend time with your mobile phone, spend a few minutes watching how other individuals use mobile phones. When you attend a basketball game today, watch what other folks do with mobile phones. Take what you learn with you to the office on Monday.

January 9

Many Americans go to Church on Sunday. There is an expression of faith and fellowship experienced by folks who go to Church. A scientist would have a hard time measuring the return on investment of this endeavor.

So much of marketing is a balance between art and science, a battle between faith (branding, engagement) and profit (return on investment measured via analytics tools).

In recent years, marketers have moved closer to art. The analytics profession was given better tools, pushing it closer to science.

Both sides, of course, are wrong. There's a middle ground, a place where risk taking and experimentation are complemented by metrics that illustrate the benefits of experimentation.

Have faith in the middle ground!

January 10

It is a time-honored tradition. Your boss asks you to identify research that confirms or denies a corporate initiative.

It is so easy to purchase a research report that confirms what you want to do.

It is so easy to purchase a research report that tells you not do what you want to do.

Today, instead of blindly purchasing a research report, ask yourself a simple question:

> Question: "What is the author selling?"

Research reports aren't freely available, are they? The author isn't doing research for the holistic purpose of creating a more viable industry. At research companies, reports cost money because the author is selling something. Carefully consider what it is that you are actually purchasing.

January 11

The new year is a week-and-a-half old. I'm going to guess that you had one day where sales did not meet expectations. Somewhere, there is an executive who wants to understand what went wrong on that day.

Where possible, try to extend the analysis window, from a day to a week, from a week to a month, from a month to a year.

Business analysis is a lot like tossing a coin 365 times. It is entirely possible that you'll get eleven heads in a row, and it is possible that later in the year you'll get eleven tails in a row.

By extending the analysis window, you eliminate business variability caused by random chance.

Too often, our modern analytics tools cause us to over-analyze events that are clouded by random variability. We need to step back, and measure behavior on a longer timeframe. If we step back, we'll find that actual customer behavior is much more stable and consistent than we've been led to believe.

January 12

I recently visited an e-commerce website that I had a previous relationship with. I viewed a half-dozen items, but chose to not purchase anything.

Four hours later, the e-commerce brand sent me a trigger-based e-mail marketing message, offering me 15% off my next order. The text of the message suggested that I was receiving this offer because I did not purchase anything when I visited the website earlier in the day.

There are two camps in marketing. One camp wants you to "convert", now, and will offer you almost anything to get you to convert. Another camp wants to cultivate "loyalty".

If you are in the loyalty camp, this promotion might not meet your expectations. After all, the promotion makes it clear that the brand financially penalizes customers who act in the best interest of the brand.

Today, think carefully about the signals you send to your best customers. What, exactly, are you telling your best customers about how you value them?

January 13

Remember in the 1980s and 1990s when NBC broadcast comedies on Thursday nights? You had to watch, it was "Must See TV", right?

What is it about your business that customers must not miss? If you can't think of anything, might it be a good time to craft a reason for your customers to interact with your business each week?

January 14

It's Friday, and you are secretly hoping that you can sneak out of the office early, maybe around 2:00pm today. After all, it is a Holiday weekend, with MLK day just around the corner.

Every hour you spend, whether at work, relaxing, being creative, or sneaking out early on a Friday afternoon, manifests itself in the customer experience with your brand. And every time that experience is compromised, a marketer seeks to offer a discount or promotion in order to recapture what was lost.

If you are sneaking out early today, make good use of the time. Be creative. Think positively. Spend time with family. Spend time with hobbies. Come up with ideas that you can implement when you return to the office next week.

January 15

You probably have a Saturday ritual, a series of activities that you do each and every Saturday, right? Maybe it is coffee in the morning, a youth soccer game, or a trip to the hardware store?

You visit brands that fit in your Saturday routine.

When you go to work next week, spend a few minutes thinking about where your company fits in the weekly routine of your customer. How would you measure your place in that routine? How, as a marketer, do you enable your business to capitalize on that routine?

January 16

Subscribe to the e-mail marketing messages of a competing brand, and subscribe to the e-mail marketing messages of a non-competing brand. Pay close attention to the strategies employed by these businesses.

In fact, you can create your own business intelligence team by simply subscribing to two or three dozen e-mail marketing programs from competing and non-competing brands. Document when these businesses send messages. Document the discounts and promotions they offer. Keep tabs of subtle changes in messaging and merchandising strategy.

Present your unsolicited findings to your management team a monthly basis.

January 17

"I have a dream."

There's a good chance you are not at work today.

If you are blessed with a rare, paid holiday, then take some time to apply the spirit of message offered by "I have a dream" to your life. What do you want to accomplish, personally and professionally? What kind of sacrifices would be required to make the dream come true?

Too often, we trudge in to work like cogs in a giant machine. We're more than "Dilbert", we're more than "The Office". We, too, can have a dream. And we can make that dream happen.

January 18

Start making that dream happen.

If you are responsible for hosting a meeting, do everybody a favor today. With ten minutes left in the meeting, make an announcement. Tell your audience that there are five minutes left, that you are ending the meeting at five minutes before the top of the hour. Then honor your promise, let your audience leave five minutes before the top of the hour.

Next week, end your meeting ten minutes early, giving the attendees a chance to check e-mail prior to their next meeting.

You'll find that you will earn a reputation for hosting meetings that end on time. You'll find that people want to attend your meetings. You'll find that people will start to listen to you.

And when people listen to you, they begin to believe in you.

You'll find that it may not be that hard to start making your dreams come true.

January 19

It's Wednesday, "hump day" as the pundits call it.

If you want a customer segmentation hint, try this … segment customers based on the day of the week that customers purchase merchandise.

You are likely to find that e-commerce customers who buy on Monday or Tuesday tend to have above-average value. You are likely to find that retail customers who purchase on Friday, Saturday, or Sunday have above-average value.

January 20

Instead of analyzing e-mail campaigns via open rates, click-through rates, and conversion rates, try something different.

Go back to data from last year's fourth quarter (October, November, and December). Measure the percentage of e-mail subscribers as of October 1 who clicked on at least one e-mail campaign in October/November/December. Measure the percentage of e-mail subscribers as of October 1 who purchased after clicking on at least one e-mail campaign in October/November/December.

You're likely to find that your e-mail campaigns, when measured in aggregate, perform far better than you previously thought.

January 21

For the remainder of the year, take back Friday afternoons.

Go ahead and work on whatever you want to work on until Friday at 1:00pm.

After 1:00pm on Friday, work on what you think is important. If you have to work an extra hour each day during the week to make up the time, do it.

You are a smart person with great ideas. Your ideas have a smaller chance of being implemented if you do not invest time cultivating your ideas.

Most of the tools I use in my consulting practice are the result of Friday afternoon research time. Four hours of research time each week becomes two-hundred hours a year, it becomes two-thousand hours over the course of a decade.

In other words, it is a meaningful investment of time, one that can deliver a meaningful return on investment.

January 22

Recently, I read a marketing article where the author suggested that businesses will be "out of business" if they do not implement a viable mobile marketing strategy in the next two years.

Horsefeathers!

Always ask yourself the following question:

Question: "What is the author selling?"

Mobile is one of those marketing channels that will undoubtedly change e-commerce forever. In fact, it may have the same impact on e-commerce that e-commerce had on traditional direct marketing.

But we're in the top half of the first inning when it comes to mobile marketing, folks. Most of us haven't even had a chance to step up to the plate, yet.

Pay close attention to what folks are doing in the mobile realm. Even more important, pay close attention to "what works". Experiment. Test. Try things!

January 23

If you sell customer information to other companies, take a few minutes and think about this activity from the standpoint of the customer.

I realize this was a "best practice" in the 1900s – 1990s.

And don't give me the "the customer benefits because the customer is exposed to products and services that may be of interest to the customer" tagline. When is the last time you received a marketing intrusion and said to yourself "wow, I'm thankful that I was just exposed to a product or service that another brand thought might be of interest to me?"

If you are going to continue to buy/sell customer information, take a few minutes today and think about how the customer might be able to share in the profit you generate by buying/selling customer information.

January 24

Truthiness is destroying marketing. Granted, this doesn't mean that we in the marketing community weren't already capable of destroying ourselves without truthiness.

So often, truthiness stems from basic, simple metrics. We measure conversion rate in real time because we can. We don't measure long-term customer behavior because it isn't easy to measure. As a result, we've created a base of knowledge that is often fraudulent. In other words, what we know is related to a how a customer responds to a promotion. What we don't know is how a customer behaves over time. It's far more important that we know how a customer behaves over time.

Just because we can calculate things "on the fly" doesn't mean that what we are calculating leads us to a solution where business performance is optimized.

January 25

Maybe you've read studies that demonstrate the value of a customer. You learned that a customer that is on Facebook is worth 40% more than a customer not on Facebook, and you learned that a Facebook Fan is worth 140% more than a customer not on Facebook.

This is a classic example of "truthiness".

We immediately believe that Facebook is valuable, based on the metrics presented to us. We immediately think about Facebook strategies and tactics that may result in more Fans, because if we have more Fans, we'll have an increase in net sales.

Horsefeathers!

January 26

Here's a little secret for you.

Your best customers "do everything".

They "do everything" not because of our own marketing brilliance. They simply "do everything" because that's what a best customer does!

Sports fans know this. They watch games on television, they listen to games on the radio, they attend games, they buy food from concession stands, they purchase licensed apparel. Little of this has to do with marketing brilliance, it's simply what a fan does.

Your business has a subset of the customer base that behaves like this. Your total "brand experience" caused this, with your merchandise being the most important component of the "brand experience".

January 27

If you want to test the Facebook hypothesis (customers are worth "x" percent more if they are on Facebook), give this analysis a try.

Segment customers by twelve-month spend, through December 31, 2010. Then create attributes that describe the number of merchandise divisions the customer purchased from. Create attributes that describe the number of marketing channels the customer purchased from. And create an indicator that measures if the customer is a "Facebook Fan" or not.

Armed with this information, create a regression model that measures January 2011 spend across this audience, using 2010 spend, merchandise divisions, marketing channels, and the "Facebook Fan" indicator as predictive variables.

If the "Facebook Fan" indicator is a positive and significant indicator, then congratulations, you've proven that being a "Facebook Fan" causes incremental value to be delivered to your business. Multiply the coefficient by the number of customers possessing the coefficient, and you have the financial (net sales) impact that being a "Facebook Fan" had on your business.

I am willing to bet that the financial impact, if statistically significant, is much less than what the pundits tell us it is.

January 28

Where possible, when trying to measure the impact of marketing programs, control for other factors.

Marketers and analytics practitioners usually fail to control for other factors, often causing significant errors in marketing attribution to happen. "Facebook Fans" aren't worth much, but "Best Customers" are worth a lot. When we "steal" the value of "Best Customers" and attribute it to "Facebook Fans", we do our industry a disservice.

When you read a study about the value of "Facebook Fans", ask yourself a question:

Question: "What is the author selling?"

January 29

Modern analytics software makes it really easy to analyze any issue.

So if you are going to use analytics software, please be willing to do a little bit of hard work. If you don't possess the skills to run a regression analysis, no problem, just segment customers by prior spend and prior recency (months since last purchase). Next, segment customers by the variable you want to analyze (i.e. Facebook Fans). Finally, do something a bit different. Pick a "future timeframe", and compare customer activity in this "future timeframe" by the segments you created on a prior timeframe.

When you do this, you control for prior activity, leaving you with the actual future impact of the variable you want to assess.

Yes, this is an important segmentation tip!

January 30

Would you be willing to give up 20% of your salary next month as a promotion to encourage your boss to become more "engaged" with you?

I'll bet that almost none of you are willing to do that.

And yet, as marketers, we thrust discounts and promotions upon our customers, praying that they will become more "engaged" with us.

We're going to destroy marketing with our lust for "engaged" customers, a lust that we're willing to purchase with discounts and promotions that erode gross margin and cheapen the brand.

January 31

Discounts and promotions are taxes placed upon brands for being unremarkable.

February 1

February is the best month of the entire year.

If you are a salaried employee, your monthly salary is spread across just twenty-eight days, not thirty or thirty-one. It's as if you received a pay raise of between seven and eleven percent!

Now, most of you are probably thinking, "well, February is not the best month of the year. It's cold. Winter is miserable. I hate blizzards!"

Well, it is the best month of the year if you create a reason for February being the best month!

As marketers, don't we have a responsibility to make February (or any month) special with our customers? What is the reason that a customer should part with $125 of hard-earned after-tax dollars in February?

We have to create a reason for February (or any month) to be special.

What is the reason that customers should buy from your business this month? What event, activity, or merchandise opportunity are you promoting to make February special?

February 2

Did you anger your spouse today?

If you did, maybe you purchased flowers for your spouse as a way of saying "I'm sorry".

Flowers are nice when offered on an infrequent basis. If you anger your spouse every day, and every day you give your spouse flowers, you'll quickly find that flowers have no meaning.

This is our modern marketing world, where we offer discounts and promotions and free shipping in the same vein as we'd offer a spouse flowers after making a mistake.

Eventually, discounts and promotions and free shipping lose their impact.

Then, what do you do to encourage customers to purchase?

February 3

If you want to see a vision of the future of marketing, rent the movie "Idiocracy"!

February 4

You have data for the entire month of January. So instead of reporting on "website conversion rates" during January, try something different.

Look at all unique visitors, and measure a "monthly conversion rate". Instead of reporting a 4.338% conversion rate within visits, you may find that your "monthly conversion rate" is actually 17%. You view the world in a different way when 17% of your customers convert, not 4%.

Remember, anytime you can analyze customer behavior over time, you remove a lot of random variability that clouds results and causes us to make poor business decisions. You actually learn that it is ok that a customer visited your website and didn't purchase anything if it led to a purchase three days later.

February 5

Conversion is an interesting concept. We calibrate all of our online metrics around the concept that a customer must complete an "action" within one visit.

In life, we don't measure success within one visit. Think about the relationship you have with your spouse. Did you get married after a first date? When you remodel a house, do you remodel everything, or do you remodel specific rooms as money becomes available?

Conversion can be a challenge, requiring many visits across multiple channels. Use integrated data, and expand your analysis window, you are likely to observe more consistent and reliable outcomes as a result.

February 6

The Super Bowl!

This game is nothing short of a National Holiday, with more than ninety million citizens viewing the game on an annual basis.

Success did not happen overnight, did it? It took decades to make this annual event a phenomenon.

What is the event that your business promotes, each and every year? And don't say something like "Cyber Monday", that's an event promoted by a trade organization to benefit trade organization members, it isn't an event specific to your brand.

When I worked at Nordstrom, I was amazed by the "Anniversary Sale". This event, held in the last half of July, generated business that often exceeded Holiday sales. In case you were wondering, it is very, very hard to generate sales in July, much less sales levels that rival the run-up to Christmas!

Best customers were given an opportunity to "pre-select" Fall merchandise at a discount before the sale began. Once the sale began, all customers could purchase Fall merchandise at discounted prices. When the sale ended, priced returned to normal.

Create an event. Pick a time of the year that gives you a competitive advantage. Promote the living daylights out of the event. Give the customer something so valuable that the customer has to share information about your brand with everybody she knows. Then maintain the tradition, making the event bigger and better each year.

This is the opposite strategy of driving sales through free shipping promotions or 'buy one get one free' promotions or any other gimmick that produces short-term, hollow sales gains. So, yes, it is going to take hard work to make this happen.

No tradition happens easily.

What is the event that you promote that customers cannot live without?

February 7

"Faux Metrics" are metrics that appear to have significant meaning, but in reality, do not necessarily correlate with profitability.

Can you think of an example of a "Faux Metric"?

February 8

E-Mail marketing is a discipline that lives and breathes "faux metrics".

"Open Rate" is a faux metric. Take one of your e-mail subscribers. This customer receives e-mail messages on her smartphone. She sees your message, she even opens the message on her phone, but she doesn't download images.

Your customer interacted with your message.

Your "Open Rate" suggests that the customer did not interact with your message, because images were not downloaded.

Be wary of any reporting based on "faux metrics".

February 9

In e-mail marketing, "click-through rate" is a faux metric.

You open your e-mail marketing message on your smartphone. You read the entire message. And, then you don't do anything.

The next day, you visit the website, and you purchase merchandise.

Your e-mail marketing team would deem this a failure. The customer did not click-through the e-mail marketing message.

Your CFO would deem this a success. The customer ordered, quite possibly because of the e-mail marketing message the customer received the day before.

Consider abandoning easy-to-measure metrics like "click-through rate". Instead, focus on whether the customer actually acted in a manner consistent with those that yield sales and profit. You can measure profit via holdout tests.

February 10

In e-mail marketing, "conversion rate" is a faux metric.

Maybe your customer actually clicks-through an e-mail marketing message, and visits your website. But, in that visit, the customer does not purchase anything.

Instead, the customer leaves the website. Eight days later, the customer visits the website again and purchases merchandise.

If the marketer doesn't extend the purchase window, then "conversion" does not happen in this framework, even though the customer actually yielded a positive action, purchasing merchandise after receiving an e-mail marketing message.

Again, consider abandoning faux metrics like "conversion rate". Instead, focus on metrics that truly matter.

February 11

In e-mail marketing, a metric that truly matters is "lift".

Take your e-mail marketing list, and create two segments. Sample 10% of the file, and put them in the "mail group". Sample 10% of the file, and put them in the "not mailed group", and do not deliver your e-mail marketing message to this segment.

After seven days, calculate the average sales per e-mail subscriber in each group. Subtract the difference. This difference is called "lift", it is the true value of delivering an e-mail marketing message across all channels.
- Mailed Group = $200,000 across 10,000 subscribers: $0.20 per subscriber.
- Non-Mailed Group = $150,000 across 10,000 subscribers: $0.15 per subscriber.
- Lift = $0.20 - $0.15 = $0.05.

A surprisingly small number of e-mail marketers actually measure "lift".

Hint: "Lift" is almost always different than the performance of an e-mail marketing message as measured via open-rates, click-through rates, and conversion rates.

February 12

Here's another good way to measure e-mail marketing performance:
- On January 1, identify any customer who purchased in the past twelve months, and is an e-mail subscriber.
- In the next twelve months, measure the percentage of this audience that clicks-through at least one campaign.

30

During the course of a year, an e-mail subscriber who values the message you communicate is likely to click-through at least one campaign.

February 13

The longer-term impact of e-mail can be measured on a monthly or quarterly basis.

Again, sample two similar audiences, maybe 5% of your e-mail list is in the "mail group", and 5% of your e-mail list is in your "no mail group".

Keep customers in these two groups for three months.

Yes, I said three months.

At the end of three months, compare the difference in spend between the "mail group" and the "no mail" group. This is the impact e-mail has on the business during the course of a quarter.

You're likely to observe very different results when measuring e-mail performance in this manner ... very different than what you observe measuring opens/clicks/conversions. You average the performance of good campaigns and bad campaigns. You capture sales that you would normally lose in the open/click/convert analysis process. You measure the longer-term impact of "branding", if there is any such thing.

February 14

Happy Valentine's Day!

If you have a significant other, chances are that you celebrate Valentine's Day.

Valentine's Day should cause the marketer to think about two things.
1. What could we do to reward our best customers, to make the customer feel valuable on Valentine's Day? No, I'm not talking about a free shipping promotion!
2. What kind of annual event could we promote, an annual event that caused customers to annualize behavior?

Think about the ways that you can demonstrate your love for the customer!

February 15

Traps.

Everywhere you look, folks are setting up traps, trying to catch you in a some dilly of a pickle.

You probably have a great idea at work, you want to try something new.

And somewhere, somebody doesn't want you to execute your new idea. That person is likely to set up a trap.

February 16

A common trap is the "ROI" trap.

Somebody is going to challenge you, asking you to "prove" the return on investment of your idea.

Of course, you've never tried your new idea, so you can't possibly know what the return on investment is likely to be. Your co-workers know this, so they use return on investment as a trap, as a way to get you to not execute your new idea.

As an individual recently told me on Twitter, "you'll never ever try a new idea if you have to prove that the new idea will generate a return on investment".

So true.

February 17

If you are forced to prove the return on investment of a new activity, you have at least three options.
1. Make up numbers.
2. Compare your new activity to new activities in the past, measuring how effective prior new activities were.
3. Use irrational arguments.

So often, we make up numbers, or we use irrational arguments. We'll spend weeks creating a theoretical profit and loss statement that looks impressive and may even convince the CFO to try our idea. Or we will just start using irrational arguments. We'll say that our competitors are doing something, so we have to do it as well in order to 'stay competitive'.

It might be a good idea to keep a log of all new activities, measuring the return on investment of prior new activities. If you have this log, you can go back to it and suggest that your new idea has a 35% chance of succeeding, and if it succeeds, the company will see a return on investment of "$x".

This allows your leadership team to consider if they want to accept a certain level of risk in return for a return on investment observed in prior activities.

February 18

If you are a marketer, then you know all about the 'privacy trap'.

Maybe you want to execute a new program. Somebody doesn't want you to execute this program, so they invoke the 'privacy trap', they will tell you that you cannot execute your program because it is important to protect the privacy of a customer.

If you know that somebody is going to set this trap, do your homework, be ready to address this concern. Compare what you are recommending to what has already been approved by management.

February 19

"Resources" are another trap.

I'm going to guess that you work at a company that wants to accomplish more than resources allow. So when you want to execute a new program, somebody will tell you that the company doesn't have the resources to do what you want to do.

Again, this is a place where you need to do your homework. Go back and look at the history of your company, and identify all of the times when your company tried something new, and didn't have the resources to try something new. You'll find a veritable plethora of examples where your company was willing to take risks, without the resources necessary to take the risk.

Document your examples, and have them ready when folks prepare traps for you.

February 20

"That's not your area of accountability!"

That's a big trap!

When you want to try something new, people will try to put you in your place. People will pre-determine for you what your job is, especially when they don't want to execute your new program.

Be savvy. Pre-wire new programs by building relationships with important people in your company. Find outside resources that can execute trials for you, so that you can prove the return on investment. If your new activity is truly not in your area of accountability, then pre-wire things so that the person who is accountable for your idea is willing to execute it.

February 21

"We need to give this idea more thought."

Sure we do.

When folks want to trap you, they'll do so by planting your feet in mud. The "we need to give this idea more thought" argument is sometimes used when there are no other traps available. You've probably done a great job of demonstrating ROI, or you've done a great job of pre-wiring the organization, or you've already found the resources necessary to execute your idea.

When you land in this trap, realize that you've probably done a great job, and that you probably have a good idea.

February 22

Your CFO plants the big trap. She says that your exciting e-mail targeting strategy must be proven via a sufficient return on investment before you can run with your new program.

Be conservative.

Especially with e-mail. Lots of folks see an improvement in e-mail performance of 20% when they begin targeting programs ... multiple versions of an e-mail that are delivered to customers with prior purchase history that is aligned with the merchandise offered in the e-mail campaign.

Say you work for a $50,000,000 business that generates $8,000,000 a year from e-mail marketing. Communicate that other folks get a 20% improvement, then communicate that you expect to only get a 5% improvement.

That's $400,000 in sales, and is probably $150,000 of profit. The program might cost you $70,000 in cost ... yielding $80,000 of profit.

Why do this? Well, your CFO will clearly see that you are being very conservative, and she will notice that you are still expecting to generate profit. She's much more likely to back your new program if you are conservative with your estimated benefits.

February 23

If you want to test a new strategy in e-mail marketing, test it among customers who haven't clicked on an e-mail campaign in the past year. What do you have to lose? The customers are not all that "engaged" to begin with, right? Chances are, you aren't going to cost your business a penny of profit if what you are recommending doesn't work.

February 24

Ok, if you aren't comfortable with testing an e-mail campaign among customers who haven't clicked in a year, then try this ... select customers who have not clicked in one year and have not purchased in at least one year! Honestly, there's no risk here, right?

February 25

E-Mail marketing is a weird channel. Those who do respond tend to reside in the top third of your customer file.

And yet, e-mail is a game of small wins. Assume that 25% of your customers open your e-mail (I know, it is a faux metric, but bear with me, because 99% of folks are comfortable with faux metrics). Assume that 30% of those who open your e-mail click-through the e-mail to your website. And finally, assume that 10% of those who visit the website buy something.

$0.25 * 0.30 * 0.10 = 0.0075$.

This means that fewer than one percent of your e-mail subscribers purchased something.

For most of my clients, the rate is much lower than that … often as low as one in seven-hundred customers.

When you read marketing literature, folks always talk about hitting home runs. E-Mail marketing is an endless array of bunt singles that, in sum, result in enough runs to win the game.

February 26

Have you ever sat down and had a marketing performance discussion with your Chief Merchandising Officer?

If not, schedule a meeting when you get to work next week. Too often, your business leaders do not understand how your marketing activities truly perform. Merchants, more than anybody, care about the performance of marketing activities, because it directly correlates with their goals and objectives!

February 27

I'll be that you have some sort of department meeting that you are required to attend each week. You know what these meetings are like. You listen to a summary of sales performance from the past week, you learn about changes to your health-care plan, that kind of thing.

Ask your leadership team to allow you to present marketing or analytics information at least once a month. Remember, company leaders are unlikely to choose you to do these kind of things, it is your job to create a forum for yourself, isn't it?

So create a forum for yourself!

February 28

Speaking of your health-care plan, have you ever noticed that the price of certain items always goes up? Your health-care costs increase at a rate that is far faster than inflation, and in spite of plenty of competition, people keep paying more and more.

What would need to happen at your company to allow you to increase prices? And don't give me that "we sell commodity products that generally decrease in price over time" argument. You either sell something, or you offer a service that has value, value that should increase in time, right?

March 1

A new month, a new theme.

This month, we're going to debunk myths.

Let's get busy shoveling the marketing slush off the driveway so that we can get the car in the garage!

March 2

A Chief Marketing Officer once told me that "CRM is a four letter word".

Now, clearly, there are times and places were CRM (Customer Relationship Management) makes sense.

By and large, CRM is a technology-based solution.

By and large, Marketers should benefit from CRM.

Unfortunately, CRM is usually championed by the Information Technology folks. CRM usually requires technology-based discipline. Marketers are often creative folks, folks who do not perceive themselves as metrics-based, discipline-adhering robots.

Given the explosion of Social Media, CRM is being re-branded as "Social CRM". Be very careful when reading about "Social CRM". There's a myth here that Social Media somehow needs to be managed by technology experts. History tells us that, except in limited circumstances, CRM did not gain a foothold, did not resonate with the Marketing department, did not resonate with the customer, but did generate profit for big businesses.

March 3

Folks are going to tell you that you need "Social CRM" because "marketing is now a conversation".

Is Marketing a conversation?

I recently read an interview with the President of the Online Division of a major retailer. This woman suggested that Social Media and "conversations" were, in her view, more aligned with Human Resources than with Marketing.

In other words, Social Media is better aligned with your traditional Customer Service department than with Marketing.

There is a myth out there that Marketing is a conversation, and that you have to "join the conversation".

You don't have to "join the conversation". You aren't going to be out of business in six months if you ignore the advice of pundits, folks who tell you that you can avoid there advice "at your own peril". This isn't a frozen lake in March that you walk across "at your own peril", for crying out loud!!

You only have to do what is right for your customer. If your customer requires you to "join the conversation", then join it. If your customer only requires you to listen to the conversation, then listen. If your customer couldn't care less about social media, then ignore it!

March 4

This whole "ignoring social media places your brand in peril" argument is a bunch of marketing slush!

When I worked at Nordstrom, we had something like eight million twelve-month buyers. So if Nordstrom were fortunate enough to have 400,000 folks hanging on every word uttered by Nordstrom on Facebook, that means that only 5% of the active customer file has "joined the conversation" on Facebook.

What about the other 95% of the customer file?

You are not placing your "brand in peril", this is a myth perpetuated by folks who have really good intentions, folks who benefit by encouraging businesses to dive in to social media.

Again, focus on what is best for your customer. If 5% of your customer base cares about social media, give social media a tiny fraction of your resources.

March 5

The myth is that you have to participate in Social Media.

You know what? Maybe you do have to participate in Social Media.

But that doesn't mean that sales will increase. It doesn't mean that profit will increase.

We always make the leap that by "doing something", sales and profit will follow.

When e-commerce burst onto the scene in the late 1990s, the sales potential of the channel was self-evident. I worked at Eddie Bauer in the late 1990s. E-commerce sales went from $0 to $15 million to $65 million to $100 million in a four year period of time. The numbers clearly tell you what you need to do.

Yes, there are a small number of e-commerce companies and retailers that are seeing this kind of sales growth via social media.

By and large, most companies are not seeing this type of sales growth.

So dispel the myth. Do what is right for your customer. If your customer is 27 years old, you might have to bet the farm on social media. If your customer is 58 years old, you might "engage" the customer via catalog marketing.

March 6

I recently read a tweet that went something like this ... "retailers who do not immediately adopt mobile marketing may be out of business in two years."

That's a myth, folks.

If you are eBay, you might have been out of business in two years. eBay is pushing a billion dollars in sales attributed to the mobile channel.

Pretend you are Norm Thompson, a venerable catalog brand. If you don't pursue mobile in the next two years, odds are, your customer will barely notice! I mean, be honest, not every customer wants to use a tiny device to buy a dress while sipping a latte at Starbucks.

Every channel, every marketing concept, everything you do is dependent upon your customer. For so many of us, we don't cater exclusively to a customer who loves social media, we don't cater exclusively to a customer who adores mobile marketing.

Maybe we cater to a customer who simply loves our merchandise.

Do what is right for your customer.

March 7

I recently read an article that said that "print is dead". The author used one example from a retail brand, where the retailer stopped mailing flyers to customers, and didn't notice a decrease in sales.

"Print is dead" is a myth.

If you are Zappos, yeah, sure, print probably is irrelevant. If you are Norm Thompson, print means everything.

Do what is right for your customer.

March 8

A CEO recently told his marketing team that they had to offer free shipping promotions "in order to stay competitive".

That's a myth.

I find it fascinating that Zappos bumps the price of each shoe by $3, then offers free shipping. Sure they do! You are paying for shipping. But the customer doesn't care. The customer gets great customer service, and perceives that the entire relationship is positive. And guess what? Zappos purposely puts themselves in a position where they cannot artificially bump sales during promotional periods by offering free shipping ... they have to grow sales the old-fashioned way!

You don't have to offer free shipping. Instead, focus your efforts on offering the customer something valuable. Do what is right for your customer.

Ask yourself this … is it the right thing for your customer to make a loyal customer pay $16.95 for shipping and handling on October 31 and then to encourage a new customer to buy via a free shipping promotion on November 1? How do you think the loyal customer feels?

March 9

"E-Mail Marketing has the best return on investment."

That's a myth.

Everything is dependent upon the metrics we use. E-Mail marketers use ROI, which in this case, is a faux metric. Since each e-mail delivered to a customer costs something like $0.001, a relatively paltry $0.03 of profit on each individual e-mail yields a robust 30 to 1 return on investment.

Meanwhile, an old-school catalog might cost $0.50 to put in the mail, and it will generate $0.30 profit. The ROI, as calculated by the e-mail marketing community, is $0.30 / $0.50 = 0.6 to 1.

Now, do you prefer having $0.03 of profit, or do you prefer having $0.30 profit?

Obviously, we want both. But don't let e-mail marketers delude you with faux metrics. Do what is right for your customer, and for your bottom line.

March 10

Closed systems are dead.

Yup, that's a myth.

If closed systems were dead, Microsoft Office would be hammered by Google Docs or OpenOffice. If closed systems were dead, Apple would implode.

What matters, of course, is whether the customer loves your product / service / merchandise. The customer doesn't care about all the stuff that technology folks love to debate. The customer cares if your product / service / merchandise solve a problem or satisfy a want.

March 11

"Multi-Channel Customers Are The Most Valuable Customers."

This is an argument that old-school marketers use to convince folks that you need to execute both old-school marketing and newer marketing concepts. The old-school marketer purposely links old and new concepts together, suggesting that the customer demands both or the customer will not shop.

Horsefeathers!

I've analyzed more than fifty businesses since starting my consulting practice. In almost every case, customers who buy from multiple channels aren't good because they buy from multiple channels. Best customers simply do everything. If you didn't have the multiple channels, the customer may well find another way to have a relationship with your brand.

Here's a tip ... customers who buy from multiple merchandise divisions are truly more valuable than customers with a single merchandise preference. This fact comes out in the vast majority of projects I work on, after controlling for recency and frequency and channels purchased from.

Use channels to make merchandise available to customers. Our zeal for channels causes us to take our eye off of what matters ... merchandise!

March 12

Customer reviews matter ... that's a myth.

Well, ok, I'm not being entirely forthright here.

Customer reviews are very important. The problem, of course, is that up until a few years ago, it was the job of the copywriter to sell the product.

These days, we pay a copywriter $60,000 a year to tell us the dimensions of an item. We tell the copywriter to focus on the specs. We pay our customers $0 to tell us how the customer actually uses the product. The amazing thing is that our customer is better at communicating authenticity than the copywriter that we pay $60,000 a year.

Maybe the myth is that a generation of copywriters are no longer highly valuable ... copywriters gave up their authority to customers who are not paid a penny.

March 13

Best Practices.

Oh boy.

We get best practices rammed down our throats every single day. How the heck does somebody know that their knowledge represents a "best practice"? And who holds that individual accountable when their knowledge isn't the "best practice"?

Best practices are a myth. They represent a process that allows one to be perpetually average, perpetually chasing the competition. Best practices are safe.

Take a risk. Create a best practice. And pay close attention to the folks who preach best practices. Always ask yourself what the author is selling when the author preaches best practices.

I don't want to be average, I want to be great. My guess is that you don't want to be average either. Take a few risks.

March 14

"Customers love discounts and promotions".

That's a myth. Sure, folks love to save money. But that doesn't mean that you have to discount the living daylights out of your merchandise in order to "remain competitive".

If your merchandise is outstanding, well, then discounts and promotions aren't needed. When is the last time you were offered 20% off on your iPad purchase at your local Apple store?

Discounts and promotions are taxes placed on brands for being unremarkable.

March 15

Optimization of a businesses leads to exceptional business results.

Myth.

One of the most important concepts we can learn is "regression to the mean". In other words, significant improvements have a tendancy to yield back to average over time.

If this were not true, conversion rates on our websites would be forty percent or maybe even fifty percent, given all of the improvements we've made over the past decade.

March 16

You need to get a head start on the Christmas shopping season by offering discounts and promotions in early November.

Myth.

In theory, this sounds good. In practice, we simply give away gross margin dollars.

Take a look at your sales for October, November, and December, over the past ten years. You will see a gigantic shift in volume from October into December. This is a customer-driven shift in business that is hard to impact, it isn't easy to encourage a customer to buy earlier in the season.

If you don't believe me, run a test this year. Give promotions to one set of customers in early November, don't offer the promotion to another set of customers. On January 1, analyze the total spend of each segment, and total profit generated by each segment. See for yourself if you were able to shift demand back into early November.

March 17

You must offer "winners" 24/7/365, as they generate the most profit.

Myth.

When I was a child, I loved going to McDonald's in the weeks leading up to St. Patrick's Day.

You see, they offered a mint shake, for a limited time only. Since it was available for a limited time only, I absolutely had to order the beverage … multiple times, in fact.

Odds are, a mint-flavored shake could have been on the menu year-round, and the beverage may have performed very well.

By breaking the rules, by offering a mint shake for only a few weeks, you create demand that may not otherwise exist.

Undoubtedly, you have a similar opportunity in your business. Think about what you could offer your customer, something that creates urgency, something that becomes part of an annual tradition.

March 18

"I'd rather use a promotion to get two customers who generate $8 profit than to have one customer who generates $15 profit at full price."

Myth.

Do the research. Analyze your customer base. See for yourself whether the discount/promotion customer is loyal to full-price merchandise in the future.

Our world rewards real-time analytics. As a result, we only analyze point-in-time events. In almost every case, optimization of short-term results requires some sort of discount or promotion. In almost every case where I analyze customer behavior over time, customers have the same annual repurchase rate, regardless of the discount / promotion strategy employed by the brand.

Our customers generate profit over time, requiring us to analyze events over long horizons.

March 19

"Because of efficiencies and discounts, it is better to send large page-count catalogs to a customer than to send small page-count catalogs to a customer."

Myth.

Just do a simple test. Create a catalog that has half the pages that your current catalog has. If the customer generates 80% of the demand on 50% of the pages, and the cost of the smaller catalog is 60% of the larger catalog, you are going to benefit your business by having a smaller catalog. You'll be able to mail more customers, and you'll be able to generate more profit.

Let the customer tell you what the customer wants!

March 20

"Google Analytics is good enough for us!"

Myth.

An entire generation of marketers and analysts have been trained to analyze point-in-time interactions. Did a customer visiting from Twitter convert and buy something? Did a customer visiting from Google after keying the phrase 'sundress' buy something? All we care about are point-in-time interactions.

However, customers have relationships that span time. We consider the customer who visits eight times a year and purchases twice to be inferior to the customer who visits three times a year and purchases once, because all we care about is "conversion rate". What kind of messed-up world do we live in where our analytics tools favor less productive customers?

Our analytics solutions must be able to span customer behavior across time, this is where all of the magic happens.

March 21

"Loyalty is the number one driver of a profitable brand."

Sorry, wrong answer.

We chase loyalty with unparalleled lust. We believe that if our customers were just more loyal, we'd manage the most successful business in history.

In e-commerce, retailing, and catalog marketing, the vast majority of businesses possess a customer base that is not remotely close to loyal. Most of my clients have a customer base where 30% to 39% of last year's purchasers purchase again this year. Many of my clients are wildly profitable with annual repurchase rates in the 30% to 39% range.

Far more often, the profitability of customer acquisition activities is the driver of both short-term and long-term profit.

Now, if you are Starbucks, McDonalds, or Wal-Mart, then, yes, loyalty is the number one driver of profit.

But if you are almost any other business with average customer retention metrics, well, you're going to benefit from a steady and profitable flow of new customers into your brand.

March 22

"80% of our orders are matched to an offline marketing activity."

Wrong.

For all of our metrics and analytical abilities, we do some really silly things. For instance, we'll mail a catalog to a customer on March 1. The customer buys from us on March 22, via e-commerce. We give 100% credit for this order to the catalog mailed on March 1.

If you are willing to execute mail/holdout testing, you'll quickly learn that many (sometimes most) of the orders on March 22 have nothing to do with the catalog mailed to the customer on March 1.

In fact, if we mail all of our twelve-month buyers each month, and we use this logic, then we'll be able to say that the catalogs are responsible for all demand from existing buyers.

Mail/holdout tests prove otherwise.

March 23

We're told that CEOs must blog, the CEO must use modern technology to "engage" customers.

Myth.

Could somebody show us a study that demonstrates a sales and profit increase that can be attributed directly to CEO or Executive blogging?

I can easily demonstrate sales and profit increases when brands introduce new products or services.

If you have an Executive who wants to blog as a form of personal expression, by all means, have at it.

Just don't expect an eight percent increase in annual sales.

March 24

"Website optimization is the key to increased e-commerce sales."

Myth.

On the surface, this sure sounds right. Even better, lots of bright folks work really hard to test different content and creative strategies, and can prove that certain strategies work better than others.

Here's the big mystery. A decade of constant innovation and website improvement cannot be denied. That being said, the past decade gave us, on average, lower conversion rates and, more importantly, flat or lower annual retention rates.

The mystery can be solved by understanding two different trends.

First, website improvements have a "half-life". In other words, the improvement works for a period of time, and then, performance slowly regresses back to a baseline.

Second, improvements are measured via "conversion", which is a short-window, usually a visit or a twelve hour or twenty-four hour period of time. Customer behavior is quite variable when measured via twelve or twenty-four hours.

Customer behavior is exceptionally consistent when measured via twelve months. In fact, customer behavior, when measured over the course of a year, seldom changes, rendering many of our fancy real-time web analytics KPIs (key performance indicators) feckless.

March 25

"It costs seven time more to find a new customer than to retain an existing customer."

A terrible myth.

If you are Wal-Mart, Starbucks, McDonalds, or any other company that you bestow loyalty upon every day/week/month, then yes, it costs a ton to find new customers.

Odds are that your business isn't Wal-Mart, Starbucks, or McDonalds. Odds are that your e-commerce business retains 30% or 40% of last year's buyers. Odds are that if you work for a typical e-commerce business, there is nothing more important to your business than acquiring a new customer.

Customer acquisition doesn't have to cost much. Social Media experts would tell you that you can "engage" a prospect via Twitter or Facebook or a blog for virtually no cost. You can execute a solid search engine optimization program, allowing you to capture new customers and prospects for virtually no cost.

And when you lose money acquiring a new customer, you have to offset the loss with the long-term value the customer may generate.

Too often, I see businesses spending money trying to keep a customer, money that does not move the needle. I'd rather acquire a new customer than over-market to an existing customer. My long-term Online Marketing Simulations continually illustrate that customer acquisition is, in fact, a more profitable route to take than over-marketing to existing customers.

March 26

"The right message to the right customer at the right place at the right time."

Myth.

Odds are that you don't know what time you'll eat dinner tonight. Odds are that you don't know what time you will go to bed tonight.

So how the heck does a CRM vendor know exactly when you are going to purchase a pair of shoes? Are they actively monitoring sole wear via your wifi internet connection?

CRM vendors are talking about taking a 1.10% response rate or conversion rate and improving it to 1.16%. That's hardly a great outcome for knowing when to send the right message to the right customer at the right place at the right time. It's a very profitable outcome, but not one that is tied to precise knowledge of future customer behavior.

March 27

Logos matter.

Myth.

Remember the melee about Gap and the new logo that something like 9,000 social media pundits hated? Never mind that something like 10,000,000 customers buy merchandise from Gap each year, the opinions of 9,000 social media pundits seemed to matter a whole lot, didn't they?

Be honest … when is the last time your company changed a logo and instantly observed a 12% increase in sales, or instantly observed a 12% decrease in sales?

Be honest.

Logos are things we like to talk about, they allow all of us to "join the conversation". We get to voice an opinion. It's even more fun when we get to voice an opinion that cannot be backed up with facts!

Focus on activities that can be backed up with facts, facts like sales increases and profit increases.

March 28

"We need to gain market share."

Myth.

I run into this bogus argument all of the time. If you aren't working for Pepsi or Budweiser or Burger King or Target, you aren't playing a market share game.

Most of us are responsible for managing a $50,000,000 business, or maybe a $100,000,000 business. We're lucky to have a 0.3% market share. Who exactly are you hurting if you attempt to increase your market share by 10% or 15%?

You are far better off trying to be as profitable as possible. Profit pays the bills. Profit allows us to make capital investments.

Why do so few marketing pundits ever talk about profit?

Buying market share when you have 0.3% of the market is complete folly. Focus on profit.

March 29

Facebook Fans.

A myth.

Here's the problem, folks, and actually, there are at least two problems. First, fans do not necessarily equal customers. Second, when fans do equal customers, do not count on "fan status" to lead to incremental purchases.

If social media truly contributed to the bottom line, we'd be seeing average companies growing by 20% or 25% only because of the implementation of social media programs.

We don't see that happening, do we?

Fans are what I call a "second-level metric". In other words, you have to do two things. First, you have to acquire fans, so you spend money to acquire fans. Then, you have to somehow encourage the fan to engage in a positive action.

I'm not saying that it is unimportant to acquire a boatload of Facebook Fans.

I am saying it is a myth to expect a large number of Facebook Fans to translate to sales and profit increases.

Take my own Twitter presence, more than 2,000 followers strong. Not one consulting project has been sourced from Twitter. Sure, I have a lot of "followers", so my presence is considered a big success by the pundit community.

Because "fans" or "followers" are a "second-level metric", the marketer is required to "convert" the fan to an incremental purchase. That isn't an easy thing to do!

In my case, I don't control who becomes a "follower". So if individuals who have no interest in a consulting project become a "follower", I end up with a nice-looking follower count that has no relevance to my overall profitability.

I'm confident you are dealing with the same issues.

March 30

"Our business model is different than anybody else, so you couldn't possibly understand how we do our job."

Myth.

If you are a member of the vendor community, if you are a consultant, or if you are a prospective employee, you're likely to hear this argument.

This is an argument used by marketing and analytics folks to artificially place their perceived knowledge base above everybody else.

Web analysts use this argument to fend-off advice from more-experienced offline analysts.

Digital marketers love this argument, suggesting that it is somehow inherently more complicated to place an ad on a website than it is to place an ad in a newspaper.

Social media experts love this argument, suggesting that digital conversations are somehow more sophisticated than the garden-variety conversation that happens in a hallway at the Internet Retailer conference.

This is just business, folks. Business isn't terribly complicated.

March 31

"Everybody is on the cutting edge except you and the company you work for."

Don't you feel this way? You go to a conference and all of a sudden, you feel like every other company is operating on a different orbital plane than you are. You'll hear that some random company generates 22% of their sales via mobile. You'll hear that Southwest Airlines, Comcast, Dell, and Best Buy have mastered social media and are all soaking in a bathtub full of profit funded by the simple magic that happens when you "join the conversation".

Life is one great big bell curve, folks. When you go to a conference, all you hear about are the success stories, the outcomes that are on way out there on one tail of the bell curve. Have you ever been to a conference that featured marketing failures?

Meanwhile, you are likely somewhere in the middle third of the bell curve. You do some things well, you do some things not-so-well.

The interesting thing these days is that "best practices" do not apply to every business. If you follow every single step that Best Buy practiced on Twitter, you are not likely to experience success. If you copy the video format used in the "Will It Blend?" series, you are not likely to experience success.

These days, marketing is like playing the roulette wheel, you're simply putting your money on the number "eighteen", and then you're hoping for the best.

Your peers at other companies are not light years ahead of you. The genius they employ is not likely to work if you employ it. Sometimes, things "just happen" due to random chance. Increasingly, this is the case in the world of marketing.

April 1

April Fool's Day.

At some point today, you're going to doubt something that you read.

This day illustrates the dramatic difference between creativity and algorithms. Humans are inherently creative. Algorithms are inherently dumb. Creativity spurs interest, while algorithms optimize interest.

Too often, we give too much control over our business to algorithms and technology. We trust an algorithm to offer the best cross-sell or up-sell opportunity to a customer. We blindly trust Google even though we have no real idea how Google does what they do. Now we're heading down the "social commerce" and "mobile marketing" path, where algorithms and technology will play a huge role in our future success.

Today, try not to be a fool for technology. Instead, try to do something creative. Instead of trusting an algorithm to convert a customer, try to use creativity to stimulate a customer.

Twenty years ago, we didn't have technology to fall back upon, we had to be creative.

Maybe there are instances where social media works, in part because individual employees are being creative.

April 2

The new baseball season is upon us.

Thirty teams have hope in early April. Each team will play 162 games over the course of the next six months. Eight teams will make the playoffs. One team will win the World Series.

Marketing is a lot like baseball. Each individual campaign is like a baseball game. You win some, you lose some.

Marketing success is best measured over the course of a year. It is my opinion that over-analysis of individual campaigns is futile, because over the course of a year, the customer becomes exhausted. If you have a hundred and sixty two e-mail campaigns, you know as well as I do that the customer cannot possibly respond to every single campaign.

Marketing is like baseball, a long grind best measured over a long period of time. If your favorite baseball team loses on Opening Day, it isn't the end of the world. And if a marketing campaign failed last week, it isn't the end of the world.

Measure success over time, not on a campaign-by-campaign basis.

April 3

My favorite metric for measuring customer behavior is the "Annual Retention Rate", sometimes called the "Repurchase Rate" or "Rebuy Rate".

This is a simple a metric as you'll ever find. You identify every customer who purchased in 2009, for instance. Then, you calculate the percentage of that audience that purchased again in 2010.

Pretend that you have 100 customers in 2009. Of the 100 customers, 46 purchase again in 2010. Your "Annual Retention Rate" is 46/100 = 46%.

April 4

It turns out that the "Annual Retention Rate" determines your entire business model.

Why? Well, I've analyzed more than fifty businesses during my career, often reviewing Annual Retention Rates over a ten or fifteen year period of time.

Unless you have completely mis-managed your marketing efforts, it is very hard to change the Annual Retention Rate. If your Annual Retention Rate is 46%, and you are already competent across most of your marketing initiatives, then you're not going to move the Annual Retention Rate by +/- five points.

This is the most important metric you can calculate, because it determines what type of marketing strategy you must employ.

April 5

A quiz.

If you averaged the Annual Retention Rate across all years and all companies I've calculated this metric for, what do you think the average is?

The answer will be revealed tomorrow.

April 6

Across fifty companies and about two-hundred analysis years, the average Annual Retention Rate is ...

... thirty-eight percent.

Yes, 38%.

April 7

Do you understand the significance of a 38% Annual Retention Rate?

If you begin the year with 100 customers, and you retain 38% of them, you have 38 purchasers.

This means that you need to find 62 new or reactivated customers just to get your file back to 100 customers.

This is why new customer acquisition is so much more important than customer retention. For most of us, we're managing businesses that aren't ever going to retain the majority of our customer base. We simply satisfy a customer need, then the customer moves on.

April 8

The loyalty industry will tell you that a 38% annual retention rate is a travesty.

It isn't. It is simply a reality of retailing, e-commerce, or catalog marketing.

The loyalty industry will tell you that if you only employed loyalty-based "best practices", your business would dramatically improve, and you wouldn't have to find so many expensive new customers.

Remember, my research across fifty businesses and two-hundred analysis years indicates that the annual retention rate does not vary by more than plus or minus five percentage points. You're not going to move this metric in a fundamental way. Instead, the metric is ultimately defined by the merchandise you sell.

April 9

Let's assume that the loyalty experts are right, that a 38% annual retention rate is a travesty.

And let's assume that they provide you with some magical strategy that improves the annual retention rate by a whopping 20%, increasing the annual retention rate from 38% to 45.6%.

In order to keep your business at 100 customers, you still need to find 55 new and reactivated customers.

As you can see, new customer acquisition is really, really important, if you want for your business to grow and thrive.

April 10

I classify businesses into three broad categories, based on the percentage of last year's customers who purchase again in the next twelve months.

The majority of businesses that I analyze are in what I call "Acquisition Mode". This means that the business retains less than forty percent of last year's customers.

When a business is in "Acquisition Mode", it needs to view every single activity as an opportunity to acquire new customers.

Granted, these businesses have loyal customers, some of which are amazingly loyal. This doesn't change the fact that the business will die if a boatload of customers are not acquired each and every year to replace the customers that are lost.

April 11

"Acquisition Mode" is not a bad thing, folks. Your business is not failing if it is in "Acquisition Mode".

Take your local "Bose" store in your local mall. You visit on April 9, and you purchase a new "Bose Wave Radio".

It is entirely possible that you won't need another product from Bose for five years. You could be a brand-loyal customer who thoroughly enjoys your Bose product. But you don't have any reason to shop with Bose again for a long time.

Bose, theoretically, would be in "Acquisition Mode". Bose would need to continually find new customers to replace customers who just purchased merchandise, if Bose wants to continue to grow and thrive.

"Acquisition Mode" is not a bad thing. Sometimes, it is representative of a long purchase cycle. Sometimes, a customer has a need, the purchase satisfies the need, and the customer won't ever be back.

Regardless, the "Acquisition Mode" business must continue to find new customers.

April 12

You can easily see how misleading web analytics software packages can be, when thinking about customer behavior over time.

Your business can achieve a spectacular conversion rate, when measured via a web analytics package. Maybe 20% of your visitors convert to a purchase --- heck, your marketing folks are operating at a genius level with a conversion rate around 20%!!

Conversion rate does not tell you anything about the long-term behavior of your customer base. If your customer purchases a "Bose Wave Radio" and does not come back and visit your website for three years, well, your web analytics solution may have a hard time demonstrating this behavior to you.

Always extend the purchase window, analyzing customer behavior across time.

If you are a Chief Marketing Officer, demand that your web analyst calculate your annual retention rate for you.

April 13

The majority of businesses I analyze are in "Acquisition Mode".

The most enjoyable businesses I analyze are in "Hybrid Mode".

"Hybrid Mode" happens when between 40% and 60% of last year's customers purchase again this year.

When I worked at Lands' End in the early 1990s, we managed a business that was in "Hybrid Mode". A marketer must be good at both acquisition and retention marketing when managing a business that is in "Hybrid Mode".

April 14

As the Annual Retention Rate increases, a funny thing happens.

Customers begin to place more orders, per year. At a 35% Annual Retention Rate, customers might only purchase 1.5 times a year. At a 50% Annual Retention Rate, customers might purchase 2.5 times a year.

"Hybrid Mode" businesses are interesting because there are so many moving parts. You still have to find fifty new customers to replace the fifty you will lose. But you can finally encourage customers to purchase more often when you are in Hybrid Mode.

Cross-sell programs, up-sell programs, new merchandise divisions, new channels, there are many ways to encourage a customer to purchase a third time or a fourth time.

Yes, even social media and mobile marketing have a better chance of working when a business is in "Hybrid Mode".

April 15

Happy Tax Day!

I'm not a big fan of discounts and promotions. To me, there has to be a compelling reason that provides the customer with a real value or benefit, I don't think you just toss the customer a 20% off promotion or free shipping with the sole purpose of increasing sales for a few weeks.

Tax day might represent an opportunity to give the customer a promotion. Some customers have a refund coming, and you'd probably like for the customer to spend some of that money with your brand, right? Other customers have to pay taxes on April 15, so why not give them a discount as a way of "easing customer pain"?

And if you make this a tradition, well, who knows, you might create a reason for your customers to shop your brand.

Discounts and promotions, offered with a purpose other than temporarily increasing sales, can be a useful tool.

April 16

It is very easy to saturate your customer with too much marketing when you manage a "Hybrid Mode" business.

Catalog marketers know this all too well.

Your customer might receive twenty catalogs in the mail. Your customer might receive one hundred e-mail campaigns a year. That, alone, is one-hundred and twenty contacts in the course of a year.

Toss in your social media activity and mobile marketing efforts and my goodness, that's a lot of contacts!

When you are in "Acquisition Mode", it is hard to over-contact customers, because the productivity of the customer base is so marginal that you'll be instantly unprofitable once you over-contact the customer.

When you are in "Hybrid Mode", it becomes easy to over-contact customers, because the productivity of the customer base is quite good.

April 17

Other interesting things happen when your business is in "Hybrid Mode".

Pay attention to customers who are shifting to new channels. Businesses in "Hybrid Mode" possess customers who buy more often than businesses in "Acquisition Mode". This means that the "Hybrid Mode" business gets to see customer migration between channels happen a bit faster, with more purchases per year providing more data for the aspiring analyst.

This year, carefully measure what happens to customers who shift from your e-commerce website to your mobile website. Carefully measure what happens to customers who interact with your Facebook and Twitter presence. Get a head-start on your competition by understanding how customers are evolving and changing.

April 18

Ninety-five percent of the businesses I analyze are in "Acquisition Mode" or "Hybrid Mode".

For a special five percent of businesses, "Retention Mode" is the norm.

"Retention Mode" happens when sixty percent or more of last year's customers purchase again this year.

It has been my experience that most marketers operate like they are managing a business in "Retention Mode". We continually read about businesses like

Southwest Airlines, Macy's, Wal-Mart, Target, McDonalds, Starbucks, and a veritable plethora of brands that are truly in "Retention Mode".

The rules for "Retention Mode" marketing are very different than they are for the 95% of businesses that are in "Acquisition Mode" or "Hybrid Mode".

April 19

The "Retention Mode" business is easily able to encourage a customer to purchase an additional item, or to make an additional visit to a store.

Think of the difference between the Bose store we talked about earlier, and your local Starbucks store. You might visit your local Starbucks store two times a week, a full one-hundred times a year! The goal for Starbucks is to get you to spend one additional dollar per visit, or to get you to increase from one-hundred store visits a year to one-hundred and ten store visits per year. This type of incremental improvement is possible, and it is very profitable.

Tools like social media and mobile marketing can play a huge role as average customer loyalty increases. These are brands that might want to "engage" a customer!

So much of the marketing literature deals with a small number of businesses that are in "Retention Mode". Remember, marketing rules are different for the "Retention Mode" business than for all other businesses.

Unfortunately, 95 out of 100 businesses aren't in "Retention Mode", rendering much of the marketing literature feckless.

April 20

By now, you've had plenty of time to identify the mode that your business operates in. What mode is your business in? Do you agree or disagree with what you've learned this month about the various modes that businesses operate in?

April 21

More than half of the businesses I analyze are in "Acquisition Mode".

This means that customer acquisition is the secret to both short-term and long-term success.

And if customer acquisition is the secret to both short-term and long-term success, one had better know the long-term sales volume generated by a first-time buyer!

April 22

An awful lot of folks promote the concept of a "Marketing Dashboard", chocked full of "KPIs", or "Key Performance Indicators".

In the old days, this would be called a "report" featuring "numbers".

You'll see a lot of new-age KPIs on a Marketing Dashboard. Facebook Fans, Twitter Followers, Conversion Rates, Engagement Metrics, you name it.

The best KPIs, of course, are those that are directly correlated with profit, metrics that I call "first-level metrics".

In the next several days, we'll investigate four "first-level metrics", metrics that won't lead you astray, metrics that are directly correlated with profit, KPIs that should be on every Marketing Dashboard.

April 23

Our first "first-level metric" is, of course, the "Annual Retention Rate".

This metric is highly correlated with company profitability. When times are good, and your Annual Retention Rate increases from 38% to 41%, your ability to generate profit increases nicely!

And when business is bad, your Annual Retention Rate will decrease from 38% to 35%, driving company profitability down as merchandise needs to be liquidated.

April 24

The second "first-level metric" I'd like to share with you is "demand per retained customer".

First, we identify all of the customers who purchased in 2009.

Second, we pull all customers from this audience who purchased again in 2010.

Third, we average the amount of demand the customer generated in 2010.

This "KPI" is highly correlated with company profit. The KPI increases when customers order more times per year. The KPI increases when customers purchase items that are more expensive. The KPI decreases when liquidation situations cause customers to buy items at lower price points.

April 25

The third "first-level metric" I want to share with you is "Number of New + Reactivated Customers".

All you do is sum all of your new customers, and add the number of reactivated customers (customers who haven't purchased in more than a year and finally reactivate themselves with a purchase).

Yes, that's a really simple, easy-to-calculate metric.

You'll find that this metric is highly correlated with long-term profit.

April 26

The fourth "first-level metric" I want to share with you is "Profit per New/Reactivated Buyer."

Acquiring new customers is a good thing, as long as it is done in a profitable manner. When this metric is well-managed, short-term profit skyrockets, and long-term profit is maximized.

April 27

Ok, we have four "first-level metrics", all highly correlated with profit. Let's review them one more time.
1. Annual Retention Rate.
2. Demand per Retained Buyer.

3. Number of New + Reactivated Buyers.
4. Profit per New/Reactivated Buyer.

If you only have the bandwidth to track a handful of metrics, make these the four metrics you track. A simple marketing dashboard with four KPIs, comparing performance this year to last year and two years ago will serve your Management team well.

April 28

Notice that I call these metrics "first-level metrics".

Too often, our focus is on "second-level metrics".

A "second-level metric" is one that is not directly correlated with profit. The majority of our KPIs are not directly correlated with profit.

Now, technically, there's nothing wrong with second-level metrics, especially if the metrics are compared year-over-year.

But when we gauge our success as Marketers against second-level metrics, well, we're asking for trouble. At some point, the CFO is going to ask us what we're doing to generate profit. CFOs are interesting people, in that they have a passion for increased sales, reduced expenses, and increased profit. Marketers, of late, have a passion for Facebook Fans, Twitter Followers, conversations, and engagement.

The key, then, is to link a second-level metric to profit in some way.

April 29

Let's say that you are fortunate enough to acquire 1,000 new Facebook Fans!

How would you prove that the acquisition of 1,000 Facebook Fans caused an increase in sales and profit?

Think hard about this, because what I'm going to describe in the next few days is a methodology that works really well, but isn't widely known or used.

April 30

A good first step in quantifying the impact of a Facebook Fan involves segmentation.

Granted, 90% of us don't have the database capability or discipline to do this, but we need to be thinking of this.

When you have the capability to do this, segment your fans into existing customers, and prospects.

May 1

Your Facebook Fan Prospect List is very similar to the old "catalog request list" that catalogers maintained in the 1980s and 1990s. Back then, customers would request a catalog, giving the cataloger name and address in exchange for a catalog. The cataloger mailed many catalogs to the prospect, until the math suggested that the prospect could not be converted to a buyer at a profitable rate.

This is the way to think about the Facebook Fan Prospect List. The goal is to somehow market to this customer in a way that encourages a first purchase. Align your metrics around the process of converting the Facebook Fan Prospect List to the buyer file.

I realize few of us have the database infrastructure to do this. That being said, we have to have a vision, we have to lead our organization toward a better analytics and marketing infrastructure.

May 2

Your Facebook Fan Buyer list presents an intriguing dilemma.

Here's the problem. Facebook Fans are often existing buyers, and as a result, they were already going to spend money. Even if they purchase via your Facebook presence (i.e. 1-800 Flowers), that purchase may have happened anyway, the customer may have instead visited the e-commerce site and purchased if the Facebook presence did not exist.

Our analytics infrastructure (especially our web analytics infrastructure) is poorly equipped to handle the concept of an "incremental purchase".

Take a few minutes, and think about how you would separate out the incremental purchases that Facebook causes from the purchases that would happen anyway, or purchases that would happen because of other marketing activities (i.e. e-mail).

May 3

If you want to measure the incremental value that Facebook delivers to your business, give regression analysis a try.
- Pull purchase data for all customers who placed at least one order in the past twelve months ending March 31.
  - Recency, Months Since Last Purchase.
  - Number of Orders, Past 12 Months.
  - Number of Orders, 13+ Months Ago.
  - Number of Channels Purchased From.
  - Number of Merchandising Divisions Purchased From.
  - 1 if Customer is a Facebook Fan, 0 Otherwise.
- Pull demand spent for customers in this audience during April.
- Run a Regression Analysis.
  - April Demand is the Dependent Variable.
  - The variables above are Independent Variables.
- Look at the coefficient for being a Facebook Fan.
  - If it isn't significant, then being a Fan results in no incremental value.
  - If the coefficient is negative, then being a Facebook fan hurt the business.
  - If the coefficient is positive, then multiply the value of the coefficient by the number of customers who are a Facebook Fan. This multiplication yields the incremental dollar value provided by Facebook.
    - Example: Coefficient = $0.50. Customers = 1,000. Incremental Value = $0.50 * 1,000 = $500.

May 4

You probably have goals and objectives that you are required to accomplish this year, correct?

If you have goals and objectives, this is a good time to see where you stand. Make a list of your progress, and where you have made positive progress, be certain to notify management!

May 5

Do you know what "order starters" are?

The concept is pretty simple. Let's assume that the first item the customer wanted is entered first on the online order form. Let's assume that the fifth and final item entered on the online order form is the last item the customer wanted.

Label the first item with a (1).

Label the last item with a (5).

Now, average the value you assigned to each item across all orders.

The items that end up with the lowest score $(1, 1, 3, 1 = 1.5 \ldots 2, 5, 3 = 3.33)$ are assumed to be "order starters".

May 6

Order starters are very important.

If you are a catalog marketer, you want to have as many order starters as possible in the first twenty pages of a catalog.

If you are an e-mail marketer, you want to feature order starters in your campaigns.

If you are an e-commerce maven, you want to feature order starters on your home page, and on every important landing page.

May 7

If you have Retail stores, you have a whole bunch of interesting challenges, when it comes to direct marketing.

Let's talk about classic multi-channel marketing when Retail stores are part of the mix.

May 8

You are probably already doing this.

Make sure that, for each zip code, you measure the distance between the zip code and the closest store. Record the distance in your database (i.e. 7 miles).

Or better yet, measure it at a zip+4 level, and measure it in kilometers if you like.

This variable is really important.

May 9

Make sure that you import distance from a store into your web analytics package, and then measure every single thing you do on the basis of distance from a store.

Be prepared to be surprised!

May 10

While you are at it, code every zip code in the United States on the basis of being "urban", "suburban", and "rural".

Make sure that you import distance from a store into your web analytics package, and then measure every single thing you do on the basis of "urban", "suburban", and "rural" zip codes.

Be prepared to be surprised!

May 11

Conversion rates vary by distance from a store.

Customers who live four miles from a store are more likely to visit the website, abandon a shopping cart, then purchase in a retail store three days later.

We need to measure things differently when analyzing customers who live close to retail stores.

May 12

Customers who live in suburban zip codes do just about everything ... they buy online, they respond to catalog marketing, they subscribe to e-mail campaigns, they purchase in stores. When you see a customer who is highly "multi-channel", don't be surprised if this customer lives in a suburban zip code.

May 13

Rural customers are really different. They're not afraid to drive 57 miles to a store to buy something. They're less likely to have high-speed internet. They're less likely to embrace mobile. They respond to catalog marketing in a rabid manner, using the telephone (gasp) to place orders.

May 14

Measuring e-mail marketing performance in a retail environment is challenging.

Online performance is typically measured via classic open/click/conversion rates.

Retail performance, well, that can only be measured via mail/holdout tests. Be sure to have a mail/holdout test in every single e-mail campaign you execute.

May 15

The amazing thing about e-mail marketing in a retail environment is that e-mail marketing actually works better than most people think!

It is not unusual to see a dollar of sales in retail stores for every dollar you measure in the online channel. For e-mail marketers, that's a good thing!

May 16

Every retail store has a "trade area", a series of zip codes where the majority of sales come from.

Obtain population totals for each zip code, there are many free or low-cost places where this information can be obtained. Take all zip codes within 50 miles of a store, sum sales in that zip code for each store, divide by the population, and then rank-order each zip code for each store based on sales per population. Retrieve the zip codes that comprise the top 60% of sales for that store, and you have the trade area, for each store!

May 17

Now that you have the trade area for each store, record the information in your customer database.

Migrate the following segmentation attributes to your web analytics platform:
- Visitors who do not live in a store trade area.
- Visitors who live in one retail store trade area.
- Visitors who live in zip codes that are part of 2+ store trade areas.

Analyze the living daylights out of this. Customers/visitors who are saturated by retail stores behave different than do customers/visitors who do not live near a retail store.

May 18

As long as you are analyzing retail store trade areas, add another variable to your customer database and web analytics platform:
- Customer/visitor lives in zip code with a store in top third of sales per square foot.
- Customer/visitor lives in zip code with a store in middle third of sales per square foot.
- Customer/visitor lives in zip code with a store in bottom third of sales per square foot.

You are going to find that customers near an underperforming store have a different set of needs than do customers who live near a highly-performing store.

May 19

If you are a retail brand, you're told that you must have a "print in the marketing mix".

Tread carefully here … print response and retail marketing are two fundamentally different disciplines.

May 20

If you are a retailer that markets with catalogs, analyze catalog performance by the following mileage segments:
- 0-5 Miles.
- 6-25 Miles.
- 26-50 Miles.
- 51+ Miles.

May 21

Catalog performance is very different for the customer who lives 51+ miles from a store.

These customers, obviously, are unlikely to shop in a store. They are also pre-disposed to shopping via the telephone.

The 51+ mile from a store catalog shopper tends to buy different merchandise, more "conservative" merchandise. If you optimize your catalog for this audience, you're likely to see performance drop among the 0-5 mile store distance customer.

May 22

Catalog performance among customers living 6-25 miles from a store becomes focused more on e-commerce than other channels.

You'll notice that customers are equally likely to shop the website and stores, and you'll find that a store visit happens after shopping on the website.

In other words, the relationship has three "prongs".
- Customer receives a catalog.
- Customer visits the website, and does/does-not purchase.
- Customer purchases in-store.

There are three areas where the purchase relationship can "fail". Many multi-channel marketing experts do not understand the subtleties involved here. When the customer lives 51+ miles from a store, the catalog is often the entire experience.

But when the customer is 6-25 miles from a store, the catalog has to drive the customer to the website, the website has to either convert the customer or drive the customer to the store, and the store has to convert the customer.

That's a lot of places where the customer can "bail out of the purchase funnel", if you will.

In the past decade, multi-channel marketing experts led us down a curious path. Intuitively, it makes sense to be as multi-channel as possible.

Unfortunately, the more "multi-channel" you become, the more opportunities exist for a customer to just bail out of the whole purchase process.

May 23

Multi-channel marketing experts will tell you that everything has to be aligned across channels in order for this marketing process to work.

I'm not convinced that is the case.

My data suggests that retail brands have customers who live far from a store, and retail brands have customers who live close to a store. These customers are fundamentally different from each other.

And that, my friends, is the problem. If we ensure that the catalog, the website, and the store are "aligned", we miss out on the opportunities presented by customers who are fundamentally "different".

When I worked at Nordstrom, we dealt with this all of the time. The customer 0-5 miles from a store was "fashion-based". The customer 51+ miles from a store enjoyed "basics". You had to market to each of these customers in a different way, if you wanted to maximize the return on investment of each individual customer.

If you align everything, the equation changes. I'm not saying alignment of merchandise and channels is bad, because it can be quite good ... but I am saying that merchandise alignment alienates customers. To overcome the alienation, you have to increase productivity among the audience that lives 0-5 miles from a store, and that isn't easy to accomplish.

May 24

The customer who lives 0-5 miles from a store is a different customer than customers who live 6+ miles from a store.

This customer is much more likely to visit a store, much less likely to purchase via the telephone, and much more likely to use the website for research purposes.

At minimum, segment these customers, and measure website conversion rates.

And in catalog marketing, different creative treatments can work with this audience ... the goal is not to sell them on-page at the moment the catalog is delivered to the mail box, but rather, to inspire the customer to get in her car and drive to the store.

You almost never hear about how hard it is to use paper to encourage a customer to get off of the couch, get in the car, drive to a store, and buy something.

I'm here to tell you ... it is really hard! Catalog marketing for retail is a genuine art that almost nobody has mastered.

May 25

Have you ever asked an employee to call a customer and ask the customer to visit your store?

We marketers are passive people. We create beautiful paper-based works of art. We apply best practices to e-mail campaigns and website landing pages.

Give this a try. Have your Chief Marketing Officer call 100 customers tomorrow, asking them to visit their nearest store. Have your Chief Marketing Officer volunteer to meet the customers at the store, have your CMO assist customers while the customer shops in the store.

If your Chief Marketing Officer is worth anything, he will gladly do this. This is "Undercover Boss" times three. It demonstrates that the Executive wants to understand customer behavior.

Phone calls to good customers generate incremental revenue. In every instance where I've worked with a business that assigns customers to employees for customer service reasons, long-term customer value is significantly increased.

May 26

If today is your birthday, well, "Happy Birthday"! Every day is somebody's birthday, so why don't we just give a shout-out to those born on May 26?

When your customer has a birthday, call the customer and offer them a small token of your appreciation when the customer visits your store.

Some of the best "promotions" (and you know I'm not a huge fan of promotions) are those based around birthdays and anniversaries.

May 27

E-mail marketing in a retail environment … now there's a challenge!

You have two goals, goals that must be executed at the same time.
1. Get the customer to visit the website and buy something now.
2. Get the customer to get into his car, drive to the store, and buy something this weekend.

I'm here to tell you that the creative you use, the messaging you use, and the promotions you apply to this process are different for optimizing e-commerce performance than they are for optimizing retail performance.

This is true! You offer the retail customer a "free shipping" promotion, and you just hurt retail comp store sales while optimizing website volume. You offer the retail customer a gift-with-purchase when the customer buys in-store, and you thump your website in favor of growing retail comp store sales.

The experts will tell you that this is fine, it's ok to cannibalize your own channels in order to create a magical multi-channel experience.

I think you're better off splitting your e-mail list into segments with consistent channel-based behaviors. Craft different e-mail messages to customers based on their unique channel/merchandise preferences.

I've observed productivity improvements of 20% when creating a segmented/tailored marketing message over a generic multi-channel marketing message.

May 28

Retail customers need to feel special.

It's hard to make an e-commerce shopper feel special. E-commerce is a cold, algorithmic experience without a lot of human interaction.

Retail is altogether different. Retail allows for human contact.

When I worked at Nordstrom, we leveraged our Anniversary Sale to the hilt. Customers gladly opened their wallets if they were given an opportunity to shop sale merchandise a week before the sale started. You couldn't believe the sales we generated in mid-July, all because we offered the customer first-crack at fall merchandise, one full week before the general public got to see fall merchandise.

You, too, have an opportunity to make the customer feel special!

May 29

Multi-channel experts encourage you to align channels, because, after all, the multi-channel customer is the most valuable customer.

Multi-channel experts do not tell you about the complex relationship between customers, e-commerce, and retail.

The e-commerce customer is usually very willing to purchase from the retail channel.

The retail customer is usually very unwilling to purchase from the e-commerce channel.

This creates a "channel imbalance" that is very difficult to overcome. This is the reason why e-commerce is just a fraction of retail sales.

For many retailers, e-commerce is a great customer acquisition channel, with the acquired customer ultimately landing in retail stores, where the majority of the relationship happens.

For many retailers, converting the retail customer to e-commerce is a waste of time and money, the retail customer simply loves the three-dimensional aspects of the in-store experience. E-commerce cannot ever replace the warmth of the retail experience.

May 30

If you truly want to convert a retail customer into an online shopper, consider the merchandise you make available to the customer.

In apparel, the "petite" or "extended size" customer can have a hard time finding what she wants in a retail store. This is where the e-commerce channel can make a big difference, capturing sales that are generally unprofitable in the retail channel.

May 31

The price points that customers purchase in differ between retail and e-commerce.

Often, you'll find that the customer buys the cheapest items in-store, buys moderately-priced items online, and buys the most expensive items in-person in stores, or over the phone with a customer service representative.

This is important, because knowing this fact allows you to segment customers and then tailor your print/e-mail marketing accordingly.

June 1

Price is so much more important than we acknowledge.

I often segment customers on the basis of the price points that the customer purchases within.

Low-price point customers are somewhat unwilling to move up into high price points.

High-price point customers are generally willing to move down into low price points.

It doesn't take a rocket scientist to figure out that as you push price points down, you create a customer file that is less likely to embrace higher prices, prices that carry large gross margins!

June 2

The key, of course, is to be "strategic" in the way you manage prices.

Duh!

Over and over again, I see instances where the average price point drops significantly, from $40 to $35, or from $60 to $53. This becomes a trend that takes 2-4 years to reverse, even longer if your annual retention rate is greater than fifty percent.

Offering value on a small number of items protects the customer file while still giving the customer "something to chew on".

June 3

Classic direct marketers know a tip that digital marketers have yet to learn.
- Customer lifetime value increases when customers place larger orders, or buy more expensive items.

June 4

I cannot over-state the importance of the last tip.

E-commerce is frequently a race to the bottom, trying to offer the customer the lowest prices in a grand effort to capture market share and drive out competition. Online marketing and e-commerce is like a grade school game of dodgeball, with everybody tossing playground balls at each other at high velocity until there's only a few giants left standing. Digital marketing experts seem thrilled by the notion of giving away an item at no gross margin with free shipping ... a concept that works for a very small number of brands.

Classic direct marketers learned to co-operate decades ago --- heck, they even share their customer lists with each other!

They also learned that larger orders and more items per order led to future success.

The best business leaders plant seeds every day, knowing full well that the seed won't begin to grow for weeks, and won't produce fruit for months. The digital marketing expert scorches the earth for every possible resource, not caring what the landscape will look like tomorrow.

Give large orders with more expensive items at a healthy gross margin a chance.

June 5

There probably isn't a more damaging metric in e-commerce than "conversion rate".

The ease in measuring how many customers placed an order out of all visitors is a blessing to our industry.

Our industry took the next logical step, by implementing the process of "conversion optimization".

This is where we begin to get ourselves in trouble!

June 6

Most of us use our web analytics solution to measure conversion rate.

Not that many of us include important metrics, like gross margin dollars, or profit dollars, in our web analytics solution.

As a result, we "optimize" a metric (conversion rate) that isn't necessarily linked to profit. We get ourselves in trouble here.

Take an industry favorite, the "free shipping" promotion. Your conversion rate is 5% without the promotion. Your conversion rate is 6% with the promotion.

Seems pretty obvious that we should be running free shipping promotions, right? After all, conversion rates increase, and that means that more customers are purchasing, and that means that our customer file is bigger and stronger.

Not so fast, dear readers!

June 7

I'll take you back to a test I ran when I worked at Eddie Bauer, back in the late 1990s. We loved 20% off promotions and free shipping promotions, I mean, we absolutely adored them.

So I did something different. I sampled a group of customers who were eligible for promotions, and did not offer that segment of customers one single promotion for six months!

Our response tests suggested that the promotions increased sales by 10% to 20%.

During a six month test, our promotions increased sales by 0%.

In other words, customers responded (converted) at higher rates during promotional periods, and responded (converted) at lower rates during non-promotional periods.

In total, the customer spent $0 on promotions, when measured over the course of time. Of course, we gave away a lot of gross margin and marketing dollars running the tests, so you can imagine what happened to profit, right?

We removed almost all marketing promotions to housefile buyers the following year, and recorded the most profitable year in online/catalog history. Coincidence? I think not.

June 8

Our conversion rate / optimization culture does a nice job of driving improvements in conversion within a visit, or a day.

Our conversion rate / optimization culture does a terrible job of increasing sales over the long-term.

Think about it this way. If I want to lose weight today, I will fast, no food, no drink. And I'll lose weight! Without a doubt, if I want to optimize weight loss, I should stop eating and drinking.

Of course, a week later, I'm dead, but I've optimized my objective!

June 9

Another tenant of conversion rate optimization is the need to encourage conversion before the customer leaves the website.

When you pull your web analytics data out of your web analytics package and analyze it in conjunction with data from other channels, you observe customer behavior that is fundamentally different than what you observe within your web analytics package.

When I worked at Nordstrom, we had our web analytics data and retail purchase data integrated in one customer data warehouse.

We learned a fundamental rule about our best customers. On a monthly basis, our best customers exhibited the following behavior:
1. Three website visits per month.
2. Two store visits per month.
3. One company purchase each month.
4. 85% of purchases happened in stores.

Those rules illustrate very favorable customer behavior, heck, there's nothing wrong with a customer purchasing one time a month, is there?

Now, let's say we wanted to optimize for conversion rate. We'd attempt to get this customer to purchase on each of the three website visits each month. We'd send trigger-based e-mail marketing messages offering discounts for customers who abandoned their shopping cart. We'd obsess about home page and landing page design, making sure we followed conversion best practices.

And we'd be wrong about all of it. Our conversion rate metrics might improve. We may give away a few promotional dollars. But we would be very unlikely to improve customer response, on a monthly basis.

The lesson: Always extend the analysis window to a longer period of time than a visit or a day. Measure customer behavior over time.

June 10

It's really important to import profit information into your web analytics solution.

I'm going to stop here for today, because my last comment is just that important!

June 11

I am continually amazed at folks on Twitter who tell me that the reason they don't calculate the profitability of their marketing programs is because the Chief Financial Officer (CFO) won't give them the information they need to calculate profit.

Horsefeathers!

June 12

I'm willing to be that nine in ten CFOs will give you just enough information to allow you to calculate profit with 90% accuracy.

90% accuracy, by the way, is way better than what happens when you optimize for conversion rate without having access to any profit information!

June 13

I'm going to walk you through a classic online/catalog profit and loss calculation over the next few days. The calculation doesn't have to be terribly hard, and with a few simple metrics, you can calculate profit with 90% accuracy.

June 14

We start with the concept of "demand". Demand is "what the customer wanted to purchase". Let's pretend that your customer wanted to spend $100.

June 15

"Final Fulfillment" is the percentage of demand that is actually shipped to the customer.

Sometimes, items are just not available, they are out of stock or some other problem happens and the item the customer wanted to buy cannot be shipped to the customer.

Ask your CFO for the "Final Fulfillment" percentage. It's a number that is often between 90% and 99%.

June 16

"Return Rate" is a very important metric. We calculate the percentage of shipped items that are returned, net of exchanges.

The "Return Rate" varies greatly by company, with some companies enjoying a low rate (5%), and other companies enduring a high rate (35%).

Your CFO is likely to share this metric with you. If your CFO won't share the metric, go ask your Chief Merchandising Officer what the average return rate is, s/he is likely to tell you. If the Chief Merchandising Officer won't tell you, find an Inventory Manager, he'll probably tell you!

June 17

"Net Sales" is a very important metric. It's easy to calculate if you know the Fulfillment Rate and the Return Rate:
- Net Sales Percentage = (Fulfillment Rate) * (1 – Return Rate).

Let's assume that our Fulfillment Rate is 95%, and our Return Rate is 15%.
- Net Sales Percentage = (0.95) * (1 – 0.15) = 80.8%.

When our average order value is $100, we multiply the Net Sales Percentage by the average order value, yielding net sales ($100 * 0.808 = $80.80).

June 18

"Gross Margin" is the amount of profit that is left after subtracting cost of goods sold.

Ask your CFO what your "Gross Margin Percentage" is. I'm confident that your CFO will give you the answer (the percentage is sometimes as low as 15% for some brands or items, averages around 50% for many e-commerce brands, and is in the mid 60% range for companies that can charge a premium for the items they sell).

If your CFO will not give you the answer, go ask your Chief Merchandising Officer, who has to know this number in order to achieve his/her bonus potential!

June 19

Ask your CFO to tell you the percentage of Net Sales that are required to pick/pack/ship merchandise to your customer.

For instance, on a $100 order that yields $80.80 of net sales, the cost to pick/pack/ship merchandise might be 10%, or $8.08. You add up the costs to pick/pack/ship the item, then subtract the shipping/handling income you receive from the customer, yielding the 10% figure.

We'll call this percentage the "PPS" percentage, for "pick/pack/ship".

June 20

The next metric we need to calculate is called the "Profit Factor".
- Profit Factor = (Net Sales %) * (Gross Margin % - PPS %).

In our example, let's assume that the Gross Margin Percentage is 55%.
- Profit Factor = (80.8%) * (55.0% - 10.0%) = 36.4%.

We're very close to having a reasonable estimate of profitability!

June 21

Profit is pretty simple to calculate. We need just three metrics:
1. Demand.
2. Profit Factor.
3. Marketing Cost.

When we have each metric, Profit is calculated as follows:
- Profit = (Demand * Profit Factor) – (Marketing Cost).

June 22

Let's walk through an example. Recall that Demand = $100. Our Profit Factor is 36.4%. Let's assume that all of our orders were generated organically, without any marketing expense whatsoever.

- Profit = ($100.00 * 0.364) – ($0) = $36.40.

June 23

Let's work through another example. Let's say that we offered a free shipping promotion. On a $100 order, we have to give up $10 profit, the average amount of shipping and handling revenue we lose when running the promotion.

- Profit = ($100.00 * 0.364) – ($10.00) = $26.40.

This is the impact of a discount/promotion on profit. Profit dollars are decreased from $36.40 to $26.40 in this example.

June 24

Of course, if you offer customers a promotion, more customers will purchase. We need to factor this into our equation.

Let's pretend that our conversion rate is 5% when the customer is not given a free shipping promotion, and let's assume that the conversion rate is 6% when the customer is given a free shipping promotion. Let's assume that the average order value (demand) is still $100 in each case.

- Free Shipping = 0.06 * (($100.00 * 0.364) – ($10.00)) = $1.584 per visitor.
- Full Price = 0.05 * (($100.00 * 0.364) – ($0.00)) = $1.820 per visitor.

That's the problem with discounts and promotions.

When measured via conversion rate, the promotion looks fantastic, heck, we increased conversion rates by 20%!

When measured via profit, the promotion caused us to lose $0.236 profit per visitor to the website ($1.584 - $1.820).

Some pundit will tell you that you converted customers to upgraded buyer status, so you need to incorporate long-term value into the equations. Go ahead and do that if you want, that's fine. It's so important to calculate profit, and so few people actually do it, causing our industry to celebrate marketing activities that actually hurt profitability.

June 25

We can "solve" for the case where the lift from free shipping is enough to offset the cost of the promotion. We just run different conversion rates through our equation until the profit per visitor via free shipping is greater than the profit per visitor at full price.

- Free Shipping = 0.069 * (($100.00 * 0.364) – ($10.00)) = $1.822 per visitor.
- Full Price = 0.05 * (($100.00 * 0.364) – ($0.00)) = $1.820 per visitor.

In other words, we need a 38% increase in conversion rate, up to 6.9%, in order to offset the cost of the free shipping promotion.

Ask yourself how many folks on Twitter actually know this fact the next time folks on Twitter begin to celebrate the joys of discounts and promotions.

June 26

Profit is really, really important.

Profit needs to be part of every single marketing analysis we conduct.

All online analytics need to incorporate profit.

If your CFO won't give you the right metrics, go ask key individuals in your company. Your Chief Merchandising Officer knows Fulfillment Rates, Return Rates, and Gross Margin percentages. Your Chief Operations Officer knows your PPS (pick/pack/ship) percentage.

Armed with that information, you can calculate profit at a 90% level of accuracy!

June 27

Back in 1990, I accepted a job as a Statistical Analyst at Lands' End.

In those days, you had maybe two sources of information about catalog marketing. You read DMNews, or you read Catalog Age, or you read both!

They were the filters. They told you what was important.

It's not like that today, is it?

June 28

In 2006, I had about 150 blogs in my RSS reader. Most of the blogs I read were written by individuals. The content, while considerably less sophisticated than the polished content in trade journals, represented a refreshing change of pace.

In some ways, the era of blogging was a "land grab", as hundreds of marketing and analytics bloggers fought for the attention of the audience.

June 29

The evolution from 2006 – 2011 is more significant than the evolution from 1990 – 2006.

In 2011, individuals moved away from traditional blogging, and who can blame them? Blogging is a grind. Today, individuals voice their opinions on Facebook or Twitter.

Blogs have been taken over by the Vendor Community.

This is a problem. In some ways, we're going back to 1990, where trade journals controlled the message, and vendors paid the trade journals for access to the population.

This is a problem, because the message we read every day has changed. For a brief period of time, the message was less sophisticated, but more pure. Today, some in the vendor community push the message away from the mainstream, in an effort to garner attention for the products and services sold by the vendor community.

June 30

Later this fall, you're going to read a lot of stories about what the Christmas shopping season will look like.

Depending on who you read, you'll hear a veritable plethora of opinions, backed by faux research.

- "Holiday sales forecast to increase by 4%."
- "E-commerce sales forecast to increase by 11%."
- "Direct-to-consumer sales forecast to increase by just 1%".
- "Social Media to lead an 18% increase in customer spend."
- "Mobile Marketing forecast to increase by 188% this Fall."

The messages are authored by organizations with a vested interest in promoting an agenda that benefits the products and services promoted by the organization publishing the research.

July 1

The messages we hear from the vendor community have become so extreme as to barely represent the reality of the world we work in.

- "Why Social Shopping will dominate the Holiday 2011 agenda."

You read a headline like that, and you ask yourself a question.

- "I work at a company where our average customer is 57 years old. Only seven percent of our customer base are fans of our brand on Facebook. If Social Shopping will dominate the Holiday 2011 agenda, what does that mean for my brand, where 93% of my customer base appears to have little or no interest in Social Shopping?"

Your first reaction might be fear.

- "OMG, we are so far behind the curve, how will we ever catch up?"

Your second reaction should be skepticism.

July 2

You should be skeptical of the research you read.

Research is valid, assuming that the mathematics behind the research are valid.

That being said, pay close attention to the conditions that support the research. If you read research that tells you that social shopping is going to dominate the Holiday 2011 agenda, dig deep to find out the audience that participated in the research.

- "We studied 880 likely Holiday shoppers under the age of 40."

So often, what we read is not remotely relevant to our target audience.

I fully understand the importance of social shopping to a group of six friends, age 30-34. I take said research with a grain of salt when evaluating a client with an average customer age of 61 years old!

July 3

You'll never read about boring marketing tactics!

Nobody wants to read about how Blair Corporation increased sales by 3% by doing a better job of placing catalogs in outgoing package shipments.

Lots of people want to read about how virtual currency will change the way users play games on Facebook, regardless whether any real currency changes hands or not.

In no way is virtual currency unimportant. It's certainly important!

But it is just as important that you execute a boring tactic that generates real sales, and real profit, regardless whether anybody in the vendor community actually talks about the boring tactic or not!

July 4

Today is Independence Day!

From a marketing standpoint, why not declare independence from the endless array of marketing hype dropped from above by the vendor community?

Compare everything you do with everything the vendor community is telling you to do. You're likely to find quite a gap!

Now compare everything you do that generates profit. Not many people talk about the things that generate profit. This is how you know that the vendor community is pushing too far. Carefully scan all of the articles you read for examples where a business generated an increase in profit dollars. Be skeptical of articles that focus on "ROI", since ROI can be manipulated. Be even more skeptical of articles that tell you that the world is about to change and you're going to be left behind!

Declare independence from the hype! Give the hype the attention it deserves. Give profitable endeavors the profit they deserve.

July 5

E-commerce and traditional direct marketing customer response tends to peak on Monday and Tuesday of each week.

July 6

Traditional retail customer responsiveness tends to peak on Friday, Saturday, and Sunday.

July 7

If we know that direct marketing responsiveness peaks at the start of the week, and we know that retail responsiveness peaks at the end of the week, why are we so focused on creating multi-channel campaigns that drive response across all channels?

Is there anything wrong with e-mail marketing messages that are designed to maximize e-commerce response on Monday/Tuesday?

Is there anything wrong with e-mail marketing messages that are designed to maximize retail response on Friday/Saturday/Sunday?

There's nothing wrong with a strong multi-channel message.

There's also nothing wrong with a targeted message that benefits one channel at a time when customers are responsive to that channel at that time.

July 8

When you look at an individual marketing campaign, you notice that you are able to "influence customers".

You can cross-sell customers on a campaign-by-campaign basis. You can encourage customers to sign up for a newsletter, you can encourage customers to download a white paper, you can offer a discount that enables the customer to buy merchandise at a discount.

Almost all of my customer research is conducted on an annual basis. I analyze how customers behaved within each of the past ten years, for instance.

Here's what is so interesting:
- Customer behavior, when measured within the context of a campaign, can be easily influenced.
- Customer behavior, when measured across a twelve-month period of time, seldom if ever moves in a significant way.

July 9

Most folks disagree with me when I say that customer behavior does not fundamentally change, when measured over time.

Folks will share campaign results with me. They'll demonstrate that they were able to get a customer to cross-shop a line of dresses that the customer has not purchased from in the past.

One of my favorite tests was executed in 2009. A cataloger did not mail catalogs for the entire year to a random sample of buyers, comparing the results to a random sample of equal buyers who received catalogs for the entire year.

When we rank-ordered the items that sold in each group, mailed vs. holdout, we observed that the items that sold best were identical in each group.

This is fascinating, of course, because in one group there wasn't any advertising, no influencing of customer behavior via print.

In most of our businesses, there is a natural "gravity" that occurs. Customers are going to do what they are going to do. When we believe we are influencing customers, we may be accurate in that we can influence what happens on a daily or weekly basis. On an annual basis, all of our efforts can end up not changing the overall outcome one bit!

July 10

To be fair, I have observed changes in customer behavior caused by marketing.

You will sometimes see an e-commerce brand with a very low annual retention rate (maybe 15%) that begins to do a good job of online and offline marketing, raising the annual retention rate to 30% or 35%.

Once a brand becomes proficient at marketing, the equation changes. You influence customer behavior on a daily or weekly basis. You influence customer behavior on individual, specific item purchases. You don't cause a significant difference in annual customer behavior, however, and you don't fundamentally change the purchase behavior across large merchandise divisions.

July 11

Once you realize that it is really, really hard to fundamentally change customer behavior, you realize that there is one important path to growth.
- Find new customers, lots and lots of new customers!

The majority of what we read tells us that if we just encourage customers to become more loyal, we'll be more profitable.

Well, if that were true, wouldn't we all be growing at huge rates, generating tons of incremental profit each and every year? I mean, we're all working hard to increase customer loyalty, right?

July 12

Loyalty experts have a lot of great ideas. And their ideas can work.

Unfortunately, the ideas can lead us down unproductive paths.

Do you have a favorite blog that you read that points out all of the loyalty failures across every company in your industry, on a daily basis?

Of course not. Nobody points out the ninety-five failures that happen every day.

But somebody will always point out the five successes that happen every day.

When we promote loyalty ideas that work, they frequently work within the confines of a "campaign". We know that we can fundamentally move customer behavior within a campaign. We know that it is really hard to move customer behavior on an annual basis.

So, again, unless you are in the five percent of folks who figure out a magical formula (or stumble across something due to good timing or luck), you have to find a different formula for growth.

That formula can be new customer acquisition.

July 13

Let's repeat an exercise I've done on the blog about a hundred times.

Pretend you have 100 twelve-month buyers, and 50 13-24 month buyers.

Pretend that your annual retention rate for twelve-month buyers is a highly respectable fifty percent. Pretend that your annual retention rate for 13-24 month buyers is a highly respectable twenty-five percent.

Pretend that you love customer loyalty, and think it is too expensive to recruit new customers.

Remember, last year, you had 100 customers.

Next year, without customer acquisition, you'll have …
- $100 * 0.50 + 50 * 0.25 = 63$ customers.

In two years, without customer acquisition, you'll have …
- $63 * 0.50 + 50 * 0.25 = 44$ customers.

You tell me, is customer acquisition important?

July 14

This is where the loyalty pundits jump into the fray. They'll tell us that if we just improve customer loyalty, then we won't have any problems.

Let's pretend that we have a magic formula that increases loyalty by fifty percent, that we somehow adopt every best practice offered by loyalty enthusiasts and our customers respond in an overwhelmingly dramatic fashion.

Remember, last year we had 100 customers.

Next year, without customer acquisition, we'll have ...
- 100 * 0.75 + 50 * 0.38 = 94 customers.

In two years, without customer acquisition, we'll have ...
- 94 * 0.75 + 25 * 0.38 = 80 customers.

Customer acquisition is still critically important.

July 15

I mentioned earlier that it is really hard to push the loyalty needle.

I've analyzed fifty online, retail, and catalog brands since March 2007. Across all of those businesses, it is extremely rare to see customer loyalty, as measured by the annual retention rate, to move by more than ten percent, fifteen percent at the highest end of the spectrum.

In other words, if your business has a 40% annual retention rate (about 80% of the businesses I analyze have an annual retention rate below 40%), and you do just about everything in the customer loyalty realm right, you are unlikely to improve much beyond 44%.

So let's say that you have 100 twelve-month buyers. Last year, you retained 40% of your twelve-month buyer file, and you acquired 60 customers to replace those lost.
- 100 * 0.40 + 60 = 100 twelve-month buyers.

If you somehow find a magical formula that is independent of changes in the economy, and you increase the annual retention rate to 44%, your business looks like this:
- 100 * 0.44 + 60 = 104 twelve-month buyers.

A staggering increase in customer loyalty results in a customer file that is four percent bigger. If your CEO wants to grow your business by fifteen or twenty percent, you won't make your CEO very happy, even with a wildly successful loyalty program!

The logical conclusion, of course, is that customer acquisition is really important!

July 16

Loyalty advocates rarely share the information I've just shared with you, and for good reason!

Loyalty advocates take a different approach. They use biased metrics to promote their own agenda.

Let's pretend that you have three tiers of customer quality. You have customers who spend $300 a year, you have customers who spend $200 a year, and you have customers who spend $100 a year. Let's pretend that each tier has 100 customers.

You've always had these three tiers, in fact, every company has tiers of customers that are above average, average, and below average.

When you start a loyalty initiative, your best customers are those most likely to join.

This is where loyalty advocates begin to use misleading metrics.

Pretend that 60% of your $300 tier joins the loyalty program. Pretend that 30% of your $200 tier joins the program. Pretend that 10% of your $100 tier joins the program.

Loyalty advocates use accurately calculated but misleading metrics to show the "value" of the loyalty customer vs. the non-loyalty customer.
- Loyalty Customer = ($300*0.60 + $200*0.30 + $100*0.10) / (0.6 + 0.3 + 0.1) = $250.
- Non-Loyalty Customer = ($300*0.40 + $200*0.70 + $100*0.90) / (0.4 + 0.7 + 0.9) = $175.

Loyalty advocates will tell you that loyalty members are worth 43% more than non-loyalty members … they'll show you that the loyalty member is worth $250 while the non-loyalty member is worth $175.

It sounds so seductive, so believable, doesn't it? You want to believe that your loyalty program "causes" customers to be 43% more valuable.

Loyalty advocates will encourage you to "get more customers" into the loyalty program, because if you do that, "they'll be 43% more valuable". They will ask you to give "more benefits" to customers to encourage customers to be in the loyalty program.

July 17

Of course, you know that this version of loyalty logic is representative of "truthiness".

Loyalty advocates use misleading numbers to demonstrate the value of a program that is not providing this level of value, then ask you to give away more profit to encourage customers to be in a loyalty program that is not providing the advertised sales increase of 45%.

Don't fall for this numerical trick.

Yes, by all means, focus time and energy encouraging customers to become "more loyal", especially if you have an annual retention rate above sixty percent.

For the rest of us, we need to focus even more energy on cost-effective ways to acquire new customers.

July 18

Here's a fun way to challenge loyalty advocates who use faux metrics.

The next time a loyalty advocate visits your company, asking your brand to participate in some fancy new program, ask the loyalty advocate why s/he is "prospecting" the product to a new customer? Ask the loyalty advocate why s/he isn't just getting existing customers to be more loyal?

Even loyalty advocates ruthlessly seek new customers. Unless the business is in "Retention Mode", where 60% or more of last year's customers purchase again this year, growth happens when a steady diet of new customers are acquired.

July 19

When your loyalty advocate asks you to give away precious gross margin dollars to encourage a customer to participate in a loyalty program, ask the loyalty advocate what discounts and promotions s/he will offer you to obtain your loyalty!

July 20

A few days ago, we talked about the tricks used by metrics experts to illustrate a significant difference in customer behavior between two customer segments.

One of the most important things you can do, as a web analyst, a statistician, a business intelligence analyst, or a marketing Executive, is to analyze customer behavior after controlling for customer quality.

This doesn't have to be done via the regression method I outlined earlier in the book. Just use simple recency/frequency/monetary segments for customers through May, for instance. Add to the segmentation a 1/0 indicator that illustrates if a customer is in a loyalty program or is a Facebook Fan or whatever. Then measure the difference, after controlling for recency/frequency/monetary value, in June 2011 spend across those with a "1" and those with a "0" for the business issue you wish to understand.

You're likely to obtain a very different (and more accurate) answer when you control for factors that are representative of brand loyalty.

July 21

By now, you might be thinking that it is important for you to manage your customer acquisition activities in a proactive manner.

Good for you!

There are several tricks and tips that have stood the test of time. These tricks and tips allow you to acquire customers that will have better long-term value, and therefore, yield more profit to your business over time.

Customer acquisition doesn't have to be a money-losing proposition.

July 22

Customers acquired at larger order sizes are more valuable than are customers acquired at smaller order sizes.

One of the challenges of the e-commerce era is the ability to merchandise your full assortment to a customer at the time of purchase.

In old-school catalog marketing, you had 148 pages of merchandise that the customer could immediately thumb through.

In e-commerce, you essentially have 1,480 pages of merchandise that the customer cannot easily see at one time.

This results in lower average order values in e-commerce, and as a result, you acquire customers with lower long-term value.

While it isn't easy to do, it is pretty important to present as much merchandise as possible to the prospective customer, so that the customer has a chance of spending more money. The customer cannot buy what the customer does not see.

July 23

First-time buyers who purchase multiple items are worth more than are first-time buyers who only purchase one item.

This is a common-sense outcome backed by decades of data. While a lot of the cross-sell and up-sell marketing techniques are designed to harvest additional profit from a transaction, the practice applies to prospects as well.

July 24

If a first-time buyer purchases two items, you'll generate better long-term value by acquiring a customer who buys from two merchandise divisions instead of just one merchandise division.

This is another common-sense rule backed by decades of data.

July 25

Nearly half of all first-time buyers in e-commerce who will purchase again do so within thirteen weeks of a first purchase.

This is another common-sense rule backed by decades of data. Customers add-on to a first purchase, or they are dazzled by the company and buy again, or they have a need and purchase again.

After 2-3 months, the data I analyze shows that the customer fades away, so do whatever needs to be done to get this customer to buy again before the customer forgets about you!

July 26

When there are more intermediaries involved in a first purchase, you can expect lower long-term value from a customer.

For example, the customer who buys from your business for the first time after a search on Google usually has lower long-term value, as customer loyalty is split between your brand and Google.

Customers who purchase for the first time via an Affiliate typically have lower long-term value, as customer loyalty is split between your brand and the Affiliate.

You are better off to cultivate a direct relationship with a customer than to depend upon intermediaries to grow your business. This is not to say you shouldn't work with Google. I'm only suggesting that it is more important to craft direct relationships with customers than to depend on others to build your audience on your behalf.

July 27

Payment tender makes a difference in determining who will be a good, high-value customer in the long term.

This one is so easy, and is always passed over by the punditocracy. A customer who pays via American Express is usually more valuable than one paying with a Visa card. The Visa customer is usually more valuable than the Discover customer, the Discover customer is usually more valuable than a customer paying with Cash.

July 28

A customer who purchases an item that is not shipped to the customer has lower long-term value than a customer who receives all the merchandise he ordered.

In essence, this tells us that customer service failures damage long-term value.

July 29

A customer who keeps every item in a first order is usually worth more than a customer who exchanges an item for another item.

July 30

A customer who exchanges an item for another item is usually worth more than a customer who simply returns an item.

July 31

A customer who purchases for the first time during the Christmas season is usually worth less than are customers who purchase for the first time during other times of the year.

August 1

A customer who purchases for the first time in September or October can be worth more than any other newly acquired customers, because Christmas is right around the corner, increasing the likelihood of a second purchase.

August 2

A customer who purchases for the first time and had contact with a real human being frequently has greater long-term value than does a customer who participates in a cold, inhuman, algorithmic e-commerce based transaction.

August 3

When a customer buys for the first time, the customer is obviously most likely to purchase again in the thirteen weeks after a first purchase.

However, the next period of time the customer is most likely to buy is often in the 11-13 month timeframe after a first purchase.

Seasonality of merchandise (or Christmas) plays a big role in the repurchase cycle of a first-time buyer.

August 4

Usually, you are better off to encourage a first-time retail customer to purchase a second time in a retail store than to encourage the customer to cross-shop another channel (i.e. e-commerce).

August 5

Often, you can encourage a first-time e-commerce customer to place a second order in any channel, especially retail, if the customer lives within ten miles of a retail store.

August 6

There are subtle differences in long-term value depending upon the day of week a customer purchases for the first time. Monday, Tuesday, and Wednesday are often higher-value days for e-commerce and catalog marketing, while Friday, Saturday, and Sunday are often higher-value days for first-time retail buyers. I mentioned this earlier in the almanac, but it is worth repeating.

August 7

First-time buyers who purchase sale or clearance merchandise can have acceptable long-term value, but are generally less willing to purchase full-price merchandise in the future than are first-time buyers purchasing full-price merchandise.

August 8

If you are able to track the human being a customer spoke with, you are likely to find that there are some employees who are simply able to encourage customers to purchase again. You will find that ten percent of your employees are so good at what they do that they cause customers to have better long-term value.

This is a piece of the e-commerce puzzle that is sorely missing. Classic catalog marketers know that certain call center employees simply do an amazing job of pleasing customers, and take full advantage of this fact.

August 9

Among first-time buyers, track anything unusual or different about their first order. Did the customer pay for expedited shipping? Did the customer monogram a towel? Did the customer ask to have a message delivered to the recipient of a package? Did the customer tweet you, positive or negative? Every one of these aspects of a first purchase can lead to a customer with greater long-term value than a customer with a generic, bland first order.

August 10

If you can possibly link website visits to first-time buyers, please do so! This is a place where the fabled "engagement" metric can play a role in increasing future value. Record in your database the recency of last visit, taking advantage of customers who placed a first order "x" months ago but have visited your website recently!

August 11

Customers who opt-in to receive e-mail marketing messages from your brand at the time of a first purchase are worth a lot more than are customers who place a first order and do not opt-in to receive e-mail marketing messages!

August 12

Track the source/channel of a first order. Sometimes, offline channels like television or radio or newspapers or print can yield customers with lower long-term value, but are valuable channels because they expand the prospect audience available to a brand.

August 13

For most e-commerce/catalog/retail brands, the path to loyalty is a long one, one that few customers successfully traverse!

It's not unusual to see 35% of first-time buyers ever purchase again.

If the customer purchases for a second time, it is not unusual to see only 45% purchase ever again.

It usually takes four, five, or six purchases before the customer can be labeled a "loyal" buyer. At that point, the customer typically has a 60% or greater chance of purchasing again in the next twelve months.

There are very, very few ways to shortcut this purchase path. Many brands use discounts and promotions to accelerate the path, but mathematically, this form of loyalty development has a low probability of pushing the customer to the fourth, fifth, or sixth purchase necessary to yield a loyal buyer.

Go ahead and run a life-table analysis of customers migrating from a first to a second, second to a third, third to a fourth, fourth to a fifth, and fifth to a sixth purchase. The probability of a customer getting that far is really, really low.

August 14

You may be surprised to learn that geography can play a role in the long-term value of a first-time buyer.

I once worked with an "outdoor" brand that generated high-value customers in mountain states (i.e. Colorado), and lower-value customers in other states (i.e. Iowa). If this applies to your business, take advantage of the role geography can play!

August 15

I once worked with a direct marketer that actively tracked lifetime value.

This marketer did something very unusual. When the customer generated the profit necessary to fulfill the lifetime value prediction, the marketer stopped marketing to the customer, assuming that the customer was "done generating profit".

Please, do not ever do this!

None of us are smart enough to predict when a customer will start/stop doing something. Re-score every customer in your database each and every week, re-calculating lifetime value. Calculate the value that you expect the customer to generate in the future, tabulate prior profit and store that metric as a separate variable in your customer database.

August 16

In B2B (business-to-business) organizations, there are other variables that can make a difference in the identification of long-term value.

Determine if the customer is a consumer, business employee, or government worker.

Identify the SIC code associated with the business.

Track the job title of the employee making the purchase.

See if the customer/employee purchases at set intervals (30 days, 90 days, annual).

Use these variables in combination with each other to determine customers with outstanding long-term value.

August 17

By now, you've noticed that the days are getting a lot shorter.

Yes, summer is winding down. Labor Day is just nineteen days away, and after Labor Day, it's all over, isn't it?

If you have a few days of "paid time off" (remember when they used to call that "vacation"), why not take a day or two off between now and Labor Day?

Especially if you live in Vermont, or Michigan, or South Dakota, or Oregon, take a couple of days off. Summer is going to be a memory in the not-too-distant future. All of a sudden you're going to be beaten up over executing a poor "Cyber Monday" promotion, you'll be driving in the snow, the sun will set at 4:20pm. Who needs that?

Take a few days off, even if you don't do anything with the day but sit on your easy chair, only getting up when the ice cream vendor drives by offering you a "choco taco"!!!

August 18

E-mail marketers frequently talk about "trimming" their list, removing unresponsive names from upcoming campaigns.

This is a tactic that I never, ever understood.

In catalog marketing, you have the prohibitive cost of the catalog (maybe $0.60) that greatly limits who you can afford to mail the catalog to.

In paid search, you have the cost of the keyword coupled with conversion rates and average order values, all combining to limit exactly what you can and cannot do.

E-mail is different.

The incremental cost to send one additional message is something like a tenth of a penny. So even if the customer averages $0.04 per e-mail marketing message, you're still generating around a penny of profit.

I tend to like profit. Profit pays the bills. Profit allows us to invest in more sophisticated techniques. Don't cut back on profitable activities!

August 19

If you have ever lived in the Midwest and have had allergies, you know that ragweed season is right around the corner, if it hasn't already started.

Sneezing, scratchy eyes, a running nose, those are hallmarks of a ragweed allergy.

You dread the next four weeks, and you eagerly look forward to the first freeze, when those nasty ragweed plants are finally vanquished.

I'll bet you have something like this where you work. You have a ritual, a monthly meeting, something that you absolutely hate.

If you could eliminate ragweed, you'd gladly do that. Unfortunately, you can't get rid of the stuff, it's part of the ecosystem, it is here to stay.

Much of what you do at work can be eliminated! Why not take a day and see if there are any rituals or routines that simply aren't needed? Talk to somebody about killing a ritual or routine that isn't providing real value!

August 20

What is the best time you've ever had at work?

Was there a time when you couldn't wait to get to work? Or you were so engaged with your job that you happily worked sixteen hour days without even realizing you were missing out on life?

For me, that time was at Lands' End, from 1993 – 1994.

I think you need at least four things to have a wonderful work environment.
1. A business problem that needs to be solved.
2. A learning environment, one where you learn something about how customers behave that few other folks previously knew, a learning environment that allows one to take action upon what has been learned.
3. A team that is focused on the same goal or objective and is rewarded for achieving the goal or objective.
4. Success that is measurable, tangible, and infectious, success tied to profit, success that fuels another round of learning.

When I think back to the 1993 – 1994 period at Lands' End, I realize we had each of these elements. I was just a Manager of Analytical Services back then, a low-level manager, but one who was highly motivated. We were asked to solve a marketing problem (cannibalization of marketing efforts), we were learning how the customer behaved, we were learning about the importance of new customers, we were all focused on the same objective, what we learned yielded increases in profit, and what we learned was infectious enough to fuel new rounds of innovation. Good employees were rewarded with promotions and salary increases.

This period of time lasted less than two years, then it blew up, with co-workers scattered into other departments and other companies.

If you are blessed enough to enjoy a working environment that has the four keys mentioned above, embrace it for all it is worth. Savor what you are going through, because these windows of opportunity are few and far between.

August 21

In January 2001, I was given my first opportunity to be a Vice President. It was my job to lead the Database Marketing efforts at Nordstrom, an eight billion dollar department store with a long heritage for providing outstanding customer service.

In the next several days, we're going to talk about some of the things I've learned while leading marketing and analytics staff. Obviously, my experience is going to be different than any experience you've had. That being said, there should be similarities that you can apply to the leadership position you have, or you hope to have.

August 22

The first five days you spend as a new leader are the most important days you'll ever spend.

Set the tone in your first five days. Clearly communicate what you expect of your employees. Then do not waver one bit, going forward.

I remember inheriting a group of individuals who were not meeting productivity expectations, and were not getting along.

I set the tone on the very first day of work, hosting a department meeting where I "put the hammer down", so to speak.

Within 60 days, six of the ten employees in the department voluntarily left the company.

While this caused a brutal transition, it was a necessary transition. This was a Database Marketing department badly in need of discipline, badly in need of adoption of "best practices". I hate best practices! But when you aren't practicing much of value, best practices are really important.

So put the hammer down, right from the get-go. Set expectations early, and then be consistent about enforcing your expectations.

August 23

Clearly communicate with your co-workers what you are going to accomplish.

Before my first day as Vice President of Database Marketing at Nordstrom, I had a plan for what we were going to do to increase profit. This plan would require individuals in other departments to collaborate with my team, so these people needed to be communicated to early in the process.

You'll find that the reason things don't get done is not the sophistication of what you want to do, but rather, because people don't understand what you want to do, people aren't given incentives to work with you, or quite simply, people don't like you and won't cooperate with you.

It's better that you identify the folks who aren't going to cooperate with you very early in your tenure, so that you can identify ways to get these people on-board or, in most cases, you can find ways to work around these folks.

August 24

Set up a time for a weekly department meeting. Hold this meeting, even if you have nothing to say! After you've been in the job eighteen months, go ahead and cancel meetings when you don't have anything to say, but in the early days, this provides you with a rare opportunity to communicate your vision to your team.

You'll also get to see which individuals are outspoken proponents of your vision, and you'll get to see who sits quietly, with a discontented look on their face. Both pieces of information are really important.

August 25

If you are a new leader, you're going to be challenged.

Your boss will challenge you. Your peers will challenge you. And your subordinates will challenge you.

No matter what, act confident, be honest, and listen.

If your enemies (and you have plenty of enemies, they just haven't presented their true colors to you yet) know you aren't confident, they will trample you.

If you aren't honest when you don't know the answer to a challenge, folks will not trust you.

If you don't listen, folks will put up walls, and you won't get much done.

August 26

Know your numbers.

Folks are going to try to use what a former boss called "lizard logic" to trap you in an infinite loop of odd customer stories and company history and faux metrics.

You're going to hear comments like …
- "Oh, we tried that before, and it didn't work."
- "I recently read a comment on Facebook, and a customer didn't like that strategy, so we shouldn't pursue what you want to do, because we want to listen to the customer, right?"
- "Who would do that? We don't want to violate customer privacy and then see our net promoter score go down, so let's avoid that at all costs."

Know your numbers.

Attach a sales estimate and a profit number to everything you want to do. When you are battered by the rhetoric outlined above, share your numbers with "the doubter". Clearly communicate that your strategy will increase sales by $3,000,000 and will increase profit by $1,000,000.

Challenge the doubter to provide an alternate strategy that will generate the same level of profit. And when the doubter provides a strategy, demand that the doubter quantify the sales and profit impact of the alternate strategy. Odds are they cannot quantify the sales and profit impact … so remind the doubter that until there is a better idea with a better return on investment, you will be implementing your strategy, with or without help from the doubter.

You'll accomplish a few things with this line of argument.
- Your foes will be forced to step up their game, and that's good for the company … heck, you could be wrong, so it is good that they approach their job with a new level of rigor.
- You will be recognized as a person who defends ideas with customer and company metrics, and that's a lot more important than a leader who simply tries to ram ideas down the throats of doubters just because the leader wants to accomplish something neat.

August 27

Quickly identify vendors that can help you, and make sure you have money in your budget to secure outside resources.

Within a month of being in your new job, you're going to bump into a thousand brick walls. Don't let brick walls stop you, use vendors as "dynamite" to blow up brick walls!

Your enemies want to stop you, they don't want you to change the culture.

Your job, however, as a newly appointed Leader, is to change the culture, or you wouldn't have been given your position.

If you demonstrate that you are not going to be stopped by your enemies, well, then what does that say about you?

Remember, your subordinates, your co-workers, and your boss are watching every move you make. They want to quickly identify your strengths and weaknesses. You want you to demonstrate to them that you are not going to be stopped by simple office politics.

You set this example in the first thirty days. If you don't set this example, folks are going to run all over you, and it won't be easy to change their mindset in the future.

August 28

Immediately upon assuming your new job, give each of the individuals who report to you a fresh set of goals and objectives for the remainder of the year.

Even if you only have one month left in the year, set objectives for the remaining month.

The objectives immediately communicate to your staff what you believe to be important.

And when your staff fail to accomplish your objectives, you make it clear that this hurts their potential for salary increases, for promotions, and for expanded responsibilities. It may even cost the employee her job.

August 29

A goal or objective should be clearly written, with outcomes that are easily measured.

For example, here is an objective for an e-mail marketer that manages a $10,000,000 e-mail marketing program.

Objective: Increase demand by $500,000 and profit by $150,000 in the next twelve months by implementing a targeting strategy designed to match customer behavior with relevant marketing messages.

- Exceeds Expectations = Implement program by June 30, generating at least $1,000,000 incremental demand (measured via A/B tests) and at least $350,000 incremental profit on an annual basis.
- Meets Expectations = Implement program by September 30, generating at least $500,000 incremental demand (measured via A/B tests) and at least $150,000 incremental profit on an annual basis.
- Misses Expectation = Failure to implement a program by September 30, or a failure to generate at least $500,000 incremental demand and at least $150,000 incremental profit on an annual basis.

Nowhere in this objective did you tell the employee how she had to do her job. Instead, you told her what the criteria is for success.

Make it possible for the employee to exceed expectations. Give the employee at least a 33% chance to "knock it out of the park"!!!

August 30

Sit down and have a talk with your compensation analyst. This person usually works in the Human Resources department.

Have the compensation analyst describe the salary band for each employee in your department. Have the compensation analyst share her logic for providing employees with salary adjustments. Make sure that the compensation analyst knows what appropriate salary bands are for your industry.

As a new business leader, you realistically have two months to make a case for employees who are being under-compensated. After two months, it will likely take an act of Congress to get the compensation team to adjust salaries.

August 31

Take your show on the road.

Schedule one hour meetings with the departments led by every Vice President in your company. And yes, I realize some of you work in huge companies, so do what you can!

When meeting with each department, explain the mission of your department. Share customer metrics and marketing strategies with each employee. Listen to employee questions, as the questions usually support the worldview of the folks you're going to have to work with.

Teach.

New Executives have a huge advantage. There is a small window of opportunity when you can set the tone with your co-workers … after six or twelve months, you and your team are going to be assimilated! So take advantage of this early stage in your new job. Get out there and take your message to the streets!

September 1

I've talked about enemies.

Obviously, your co-workers aren't enemies, they're co-workers!

Unfortunately, your co-workers do not have objectives that are aligned with your objectives, in most cases. Or when objectives are aligned, the objectives create competition.

At some point in the first few months as a new Leader, you will identify somebody who isn't on your side.

The database marketer / web analyst / business intelligence expert will likely identify somebody in the information technology department who has a different vision for how things should be done.

The marketing Executive is going to run across a veritable plethora of "pseudo-marketers", folks who think they know marketing because they've also shopped in a store or purchased something online or because they have a presence on Facebook they believe they are social media experts.

A frank, honest discussion needs to happen with these individuals, early in your tenure as a new leader.

I was a statistical analyst back in the early 1990s, when Lands' End hired a new VP of Information Technology. This individual had good intentions, and wanted to encourage the use of new software, software endorsed by the information technology team.

My boss executed a unique experiment. He asked me to run a query using SPSS (a statistical software application now owned by IBM). It took me about 3-4 hours (this was 1992, it would take 3-4 minutes today) to run the query and obtain an answer.

My boss asked the VP of Information Technology to find his best staffer, and have that individual run the query using software endorsed by the information technology team.

It took about 30 days for the IT team to obtain the answer to the query.

We didn't have a single discussion about using a different software application after the end of the experiment!

Nip these challenges in the bud early in your tenure.

September 2

Create a career path for your staff.

A new leader is likely to be asked, "What do I have to do to earn a promotion?"

Your goals and objectives form a good start.

The career path is an important second step. Employees should not get the impression that if they do three simple tasks, they will unseat you as a newly minted Vice President!

Be careful with how you communicate this to your team.

I once had an employee who said the following: "... tell me the three or four things that I need to do to be promoted, then I'll do the three or four things, and then you will promote me, ok?" This individual thought that promotions were achieved after accomplishing a simple set of instructions.

It is my opinion that promotions are achieved after a prolonged period of brilliance that generates sales and profit increases, coupled with an ability to work well with others, and an ability to have a vision for the future.

Paint this picture for your team early in your tenure. Employees intuitively know that a new leader is likely to see the world in a different way than the prior leader. Employees will try to take advantage of this situation, attempting to better their lot in life. You can't blame your employees for trying!

September 3

If you didn't already know this, your relationship with your boss is really important!

Very early in your tenure as a new leader, identify the depth of communication required with your boss.

I've worked with CEOs who only want to know when a catastrophe happens.

I've worked with CEOs who audit the formulas that populate every single cell in a spreadsheet created by a member of my team.

Knowing where your boss stands on this spectrum will save you a lot of heartache.

September 4

Early in your tenure, a subset of your employees are going to challenge you.

The challenge is subtle. You might ask members of your team to analyze a marketing campaign, and you might have ideas about how the analysis should be done. When you review the final report, you notice that the team didn't do anything the way you asked them to do it.

There are at least three reasons why some members of your team will do this.
1. You failed to clearly communicate what you wanted.
2. Your team thinks there is a better way to do the task.
3. Your team doesn't respect you.

If your team doesn't respect you, you have a small window of time to correct this problem. Respect is earned, so it is imperative that you demonstrate that your methodology is equal or better than what is being done. It is important that you demonstrate this fact in a diplomatic manner … let the data/facts speak for themselves.

It is also important that you listen. You aren't a dictator, so be willing to listen to other ideas that may be better than yours. And if somebody has an idea that is better than yours, shout it to the Heavens, reward folks who innovate!

Respect is a tough nut to crack, folks.

September 5

A new leader is likely to find three groups of employees.
   1. A third of your employees will immediately follow you.
   2. A third of your employees are waiting to cast judgment on you.
   3. A third of your employees are not on your side.

Which group of employees are most important to your success?

Yes, that's right, the group of employees most important to your success are those waiting to cast judgment on you.

This group of employees are like "independent voters" in an election, they will side with the third of employees "who have momentum".

Identify this third of your employee base, and spend a disproportionate amount of time with them. Have this group work on projects with the third of your team that is on your side. Demonstrate to the group that is against you that it's better to get on board now than to be isolated later.

September 6

Eventually, things are going to come to a head.

An employee will demand to meet with you in private. He will ask you to restore things to the way they were prior to your arrival. He will claim that you are making mistakes that are likely to hurt the business. He will claim that other employees are talking about you, and they aren't saying nice things about you!

You might feel insecure, threatened, uncomfortable.

Act like you are one-hundred percent confident!

Clearly communicate that the train has left the station, that the employee can get on board, or the employee can choose to leave the company.

The employee is going to appear "shocked", after all, the employee feels that his contributions are so critically important to the success of the company that he cannot possibly be asked to voluntarily leave the company!!

Make it clear that the employee should leave the company if the employee doesn't like the direction you are taking the department in.

September 7

Be willing to have employees quit on you.

Employees quit on you in several ways.

Some will literally quit, they believe that their departure will create a swirling vortex that the brand will never recover from. I know this is true, I've quit companies possessing this very belief!

Some will begin to work on projects in secret. They will find business leaders that disagree with you, and they will, in private, work on projects that support a different business leader instead of working on your projects.

Some will move into "gossip mode". We've all seen this happen. They will gather for lunch with two or three dissenters and they will provide a "CNN-style" analysis on how your initiatives are likely to fail. When you walk by, they will become quiet, their faces will redden.

Identify the employees who are quitting on you. Have an honest discussion with them about why they are quitting on you. Encourage those who appear "hopeless" to literally quit, encourage them to find work at another company.

September 8

Have a succession plan in place.

Early in your tenure, a subset of employees are likely to quit. They simply won't agree with the direction you are taking your department in (and this is your department, folks, always remember that, you are being paid to lead a department, you are not being paid to foster a working democracy).

They will quit.

I had six in ten employees quit in an eight week stretch when I became Vice President of Database Marketing at Nordstrom. Was that painful? Absolutely. Did I doubt everything I was doing? Yes! Was it a necessary process that I had to go through in order to have a department that was going to do great things in a couple of years? Certainly.

Your succession plan includes identification of internal employees who are talented and supportive of your initiatives. Your succession plan includes external employees proficient in areas that your company needs to succeed.

Have a plan. Be ready to execute it, because folks are going to quit.

September 9

You're going to run into instances where employees quit, and put interesting conditions upon you when they quit.

I once had an employee who gave six weeks of notice when resigning. In the next twenty minutes, I heard every reason why I was the worst boss in history.

Needless to say, this employee was not given the opportunity to soldier on for another six weeks.

Have consistent and fair rules. Do not let somebody hijack your department for any period of time.

September 10

Believe it or not, there are ideas that are not "culturally appropriate".

The punditocracy will tell you exactly how to serve the customer. If you just follow their rules, all customers will be happy, and all brands will thrive in today's rapidly changing consumer marketplace.

Your staff are going to have a lot of ideas as well. Some are great ideas that you will implement. Some of the ideas are ahead of their time. Some of the ideas aren't so great.

Your job is to filter through the ideas and determine those that are culturally appropriate. If you work at Burger King, it may not be culturally appropriate to offer cotton candy as a menu item. You get to make that decision.

In your first month or two on the job, your employees are going to pay close attention to your decisions, your decisions will shape their view of what is going to be "culturally appropriate".

September 11

You have a responsibility to differentiate the importance of events.

On a Friday afternoon at 4:00pm, it might be fine to let employees head home early for the weekend.

On a Tuesday afternoon at 2:35pm, it is not unreasonable question the motives of an employee who just took a three hour lunch for the third day in a row.

And when a national disaster is unfolding in front of your eyes, it is perfectly acceptable to suspend work and offer compassion to your team … your inter-department task force meeting can wait.

September 12

Maybe you've been in your job for six months, now, and it is time to give a mid-year performance review.

Contrary to your instincts, this process is important.

See, you have pre-conceived notions about the quality of each and every one of your direct reports. It's a good idea to compare your pre-conceived notions against performance standards that you created when you accepted your new role.

One of your direct reports might not think the way you think. But if she is meeting or exceeding the goals and objectives that you gave here, well, what more could you want?

September 13

That's right, people are different.

Really, really different. Every single one of them.

The punditocracy wants all of us to be the same.
- "Join the conversation".
- "E-mail marketing is all about relevancy."
- "Print is dead".
- "Test, #measure, optimize."
- "A modern vision of one-to-one marketing."
- "82% of consumers long for personalized, trigger-based CRM-fueled messages."
- "Brand that don't listen to customers will be dead in two years."

Maybe the hardest thing you'll deal with is not finding new ways to prove that "marketing = conversations", though that might be hard to prove.

Maybe the hardest thing you'll deal with is the realization that all people are different.

September 14

Once you realize that people are different, you realize that people aren't perfect.

This is where the fun starts!

September 15

Celebrate small victories.

It is rare that one of the folks you lead will hit a home run. More common is a bunt single, of course. One of your staffers will figure out how to add a field to the customer database, for instance. It's a small victory.

Celebrate small victories.

One of your staffers will increase the performance of an e-mail campaign from $0.11 per recipient to $0.12 per recipient.

Celebrate small victories.

One of your staffers will figure out via an A/B test that customers are more responsive to a Verdana font than a Times New Roman font.

Celebrate small victories.

One of your staffers will figure out that everybody loves Peanut Butter M&Ms.

Celebrate small victories.

September 16

Why?

This is the question that a statistical analyst kept asking me when I was given my first job managing people.

I'd explain a process that we executed to score our customer file for a future catalog mailing, and all I'd hear from this individual is the following question:

Why?

When folks ask this question, they may not understand what you are doing, or they may question why the heck you are doing what you are doing!

Each version of the question requires a different style of management. Figure out which version of "why" your employee is asking you!

September 17

"Why do companies keep spamming me?"

That's the question a person on Twitter recently asked me.

Your e-mail marketing program has multiple objectives.
- Generate Sales.
- Generate Profit.

The experts believe that your program has multiple objectives.
- Personalized, timely, relevant messages.

- Reduced frequency that minimizes your opt-out rate.
- Trigger-based campaigns that maximize a one-to-one relationship.
- Getting a message into your in-box.
- Getting your messages white-listed.

The reason companies spam people is that it is the sole objective of a company to generate sales, and to generate profit. That's it. 95% of companies are going to take the easiest and most cost-effective route to generating sales, and to increasing profit.

As a business leader, you have to balance the organizational lust for sales/profit with the hard-to-execute and potentially expensive and time consuming tactics that may or may not lead to long-term profit.

You can do both!

September 18

How much profit is generated by the marketing activities you are responsible for?

How much incremental profit did you generate because of the job you do?

How much profit would be lost if your job were eliminated?

You absolutely have to know the answers to these questions.

I used to maintain a scorecard that outlined the profit generated by every single activity in my department. If we caused an increase in e-mail marketing performance of 20%, I immediately knew that this yielded $30,000,000 sales and $10,000,000 profit.

You don't get asked to downsize your department very often when you can prove that your team added $10,000,000 profit last year.

September 19

Share company profitability with every employee.

I can hear the moans now. You'll say that your CFO doesn't let anybody know how profitable the company really is.

If that's the case, then figure out how the heck to build a relationship with your CFO, so that you can share this information with each employee.

Honestly, your employees want to help.

They'll understand why you are rationing pencils and notepads if you tell them that sales declined from $50,000,000 to $40,000,000 last year, causing a $3,000,000 annual profit to become a $1,000,000 loss.

September 20

New ideas are a good thing.

I worked for a year at Avenue A, back in 2000. Every idea was a new idea! It was an amazing environment, one where there was no company history, one where "we tried that and it didn't work" didn't exist yet!

I worked at Lands' End, Eddie Bauer, and Nordstrom, companies with an aggregate two-hundred plus years of history. I cannot tell you how often I heard "we tried that and it didn't work" or "you don't understand our culture, this is how we do things around here."

It's been my experience that a combination of tradition and new ideas yields sales growth and profit improvement.

As a new leader, take a look at your team. If every person has been with the company for five or ten years, find ways to inject "newness" into your department. You need both tradition and newness.

September 21

"We don't have the resources to do that."

The new Leader is going to run head-first into this argument over and over and over again.

There's two reasons why this statement is issued so often.
1. There truly aren't any resources available to do something.
2. The person issuing the statement has zero interest in working on what you are asking the individual to work on.

If you sense that the other party doesn't want to work on your project, you have several choices.

1. Hire an outside resource to work on this for you.
2. Offer to take something away, so that the other party works on your project.

I always go with option two. If this is something that is really important to me, I'm going to lower the priority of another initiative.

This makes things interesting, because now the other party has the resources to do what you want done. If the other party still refuses to work on your initiative, well, then, you've certainly learned something about the other party, haven't you?

September 22

"We'll put it on the book of work, and prioritize it."

We talked about this earlier. A new business Leader will hear this one a lot. It means that somebody doesn't want to say "no" to you. It also means that they are clearly telling you that they'd rather work on eight or nine other projects than the project you work on.

A new analytics or marketing business leader is well-served by making sure there is money to spend on various products and services.

If your IT team won't allocate the resources you need, tell them you're sending your database to Webtrends, or Omniture, or Unica, or Coremetrics, or Epsilon, or Acxiom, or Experian, or anybody else.

If you are a marketer, then there's no shortage of agencies who would be happy to both host your data and, more importantly, analyze your data for you.

Early in your tenure, you have to take a stand against inertia.

September 23

"You'll never …"

Finish the sentence however you'd like to finish it.

You hear this garbage every single day, and you hear it more often as a new Leader.

I recall sitting with my advisor in college, a few months shy of graduation. He asked me what I wanted to do next. I told him I was going to get a job. He told me I'd never get a job with a BS in Statistics.

You wonder why a University would even offer the degree if you couldn't get a job after earning the degree?

Needless to say, I've been employed, non-stop in fact, since nine weeks after Graduation Day.

You're going to deal with this, especially from your peers. They will tell you that the CEO will never let you do what you want to do. They will tell you that the CFO won't spend money on anything that doesn't deliver an immediate return on investment. They will tell you that the Chief Merchandising Officer decides what goes in an e-mail marketing campaign, not you.

You get the picture.

Do not let "them" define "you". Create a vision. Communicate your vision. Execute against your vision.

September 24

In case you haven't noticed, it is Fall.

The days are getting exponentially shorter.

And the amount of time you have to prepare for the Christmas shopping season is winding down as well.

I realize that you don't have many options left to impact Christmas with print marketing.

Online, it's a different story. The next six or seven weeks represent a great opportunity to acquire new customers, new customers that have a reasonable chance of purchasing again during the Christmas season.

This is a strategy that was mentioned earlier, a strategy that you almost never hear online marketing experts talk about. When you realize that most online measurement techniques focus on "conversion", then you aren't surprised that folks miss out on the subtleties of customer management. You can't possibly see that newly acquired customers is likely to buy again in the next eight weeks if you are measuring "conversion".

September 25

Web analytics experts communicate with each other via the hashtag "#measure". This means that you can follow what these individuals like to talk about by tracking the #measure hashtag.

The absolute best thing about the #measure community is their passion. I don't recall seeing a group of analytically minded individuals ever being so thrilled about analyzing customer behavior, about communicating results, about wanting to learn what works and what doesn't work.

This group of individuals have a passion that has been missing from the classic business intelligence community.

September 26

I'm more of an old-school analytics maven. I don't have the passion for web analytics that the #measure community has.

I do have a passion for understanding customer behavior. I've learned that customer behavior is best measured over a long period of time … a month, a quarter, a season, or a year.

It's been really interesting to watch the #measure community evolve their thinking over time. Bit by bit, piece by piece, they are slowly figuring out that website optimization (measured via conversion) and A/B testing and tracking keywords is not fully satisfying. You read it in each additional tweet, in every single comment demanding additional knowledge from the community.

This is a great sign!

September 27

You know that this focus on measuring "conversion" isn't all it is cracked-up to be when you actually look at the facts.

- "If we've made so many improvements to the website, then why aren't sales increasing faster?"

- "If we've learned so much about optimizing website performance via A/B testing and multivariate testing, then why aren't conversion rates improving?"
- "If all of these new marketing tactics work so amazingly well, then why is the conversion rate for all of these new marketing tactics so amazingly low?"

Yup, there's either something wrong with all of the new marketing tactics, or there's something wrong with how we measure everything.

Or there's something wrong with both!

September 28

The catalog marketer has an advantage over the online marketer.

Perspective.

That's right. The catalog marketer can go back to 1990 (or 1970), and tell you how customers behaved "back in the day".

The online marketer, if lucky, can go back to 1995.

The social media marketer can go back to 2003, if lucky.

The mobile marketer can go back to 2007.

September 29

Perspective is really important in marketing. Perspective enables patience. Perspective enables a comparison of similar situations that span a long period of time.

The catalog marketer has this. Back in 1990, the catalog marketer knew that 45% of 1989 buyers purchased again in 1990. The catalog marketer knew that retention came from organic brand loyalty, and retention came from maybe fifteen catalog mailings per year.

In other words, the catalog marketer divided a 45% retention rate by maybe 15 catalog marketing activities.

September 30

Online, social, and mobile marketers do not necessarily have perspective. Perspective, of course, is earned.

Perspective is being earned in these disciplines.

Today, the very same brand has a 45% retention rate. But the brand divides this retention rate by 15 annual catalog marketing activities, 115 annual e-mail marketing campaigns, 75 different free shipping or 20% off promotions, a half-dozen micro-sites, 75,000 keyword combinations, 27,000 Facebook Fans, 11,800 Twitter Followers, 18 Foresquare promotions, a mobile website operating across Apple and Android platforms, two dozen key landing pages, a clearance website, an outlet website, 886 affiliate marketing partners, and whatever other marketing initiative you can think of.

The online/social/mobile marketer doesn't even have time for perspective!

In the example I outline above, a 45% Annual Repurchase Rate must be allocated across 250 marketing campaigns, 800+ affiliates, 75,000 keywords, and almost 39,000 Facebook/Twitter advocates.

Given this daunting challenge, what do online/social/mobile marketers do?

They don't yearn for perspective.

Instead, they attempt to "attribute" orders across marketing channels.

Oh boy.

October 1

I will say this. Attributing orders across marketing efforts is probably better than doing nothing, and is probably better than measuring the last click.

Outside of that, the practice represents a modern version of "Fool's Gold".

Computer algorithms do a nice job of attempting to solve this problem, but the best they can do is "attempt" to solve the problem.

Let's work through a few examples.

October 2

A customer was acquired by your catalog division in June 2011. This customer becomes a Facebook Fan in August 2011. This customer receives a catalog on September 9, 2011, receives three e-mail marketing campaigns between 9/10/2011 and 9/19/2011, and purchases merchandise from your website on September 26, 2011.

Who gets credit for the order?

October 3

A customer receives an e-mail marketing campaign on September 26, visits Google on September 27 and enters a brand-related keyword to arrive at your website, and purchases later that day.

Who gets credit for the order?

October 4

A customer arrives at your website with a referring URL from Twitter, places one item in her shopping cart, and does not buy anything. You send the customer a trigger-based shopping cart e-mail marketing message, offering free shipping if the customer buys the item in the shopping cart. The customer buys the item in the shopping cart.

Who gets credit for the order? Twitter? Trigger-based e-mail? The free shipping promotion?

October 5

If you ask ten "attribution experts" to parse these orders across the marketing activities that may/may-not have caused the order, you will get exactly ten different answers.

That's the problem, folks.

Anything that you want to analyze with certainty cannot yield a different answer when a different marketing expert analyzes the information.

October 6

There are ways to improve your ability to attribute orders to the marketing activities that truly caused the order to happen.

If you are a catalog marketer, you must execute holdout groups. Sample part of your twelve-month buyer file, and do not mail that part of the file a catalog for a quarter, a season, or a year.

Measure the difference in spend, especially online, when you don't mail a catalog. This is critically important, because you'll notice that your attribution routine (called "matchback" in catalog marketing circles) clearly over-states the importance of a catalog. You'll learn that you attribute a percentage of online orders, maybe 20%, maybe 50%, maybe 80%, never 100%, back to catalog marketing activities.

October 7

Another way to improve attribution accuracy is to execute e-mail mail/holdout tests.

This is something that I've never understood. Catalog marketers, by and large, are willing to execute holdout groups from time to time. E-mail marketers, however, are generally unwilling to execute holdout groups.

"We'll lose sales if we do that!"

Will you?

I've witnessed e-mail holdout tests that result in no lost sales whatsoever, in other words, the e-mail marketing campaign is simply cannibalizing other marketing activities.

And I've measured e-mail holdout tests that prove that e-mail marketing is actually twice as effective as measured via classic metrics.

So holdout tests are very important, in both e-mail marketing and catalog marketing.

October 8

If you want to improve your attribution methodology, be willing to execute holdouts in display ads.

Use geography to execute holdout groups, or work with your vendor to execute holdout groups.

You overlay that information with e-mail holdouts and catalog holdouts, and you've really got something!

October 9

Search is a tougher attribution nut to crack.

In reality, it's more interesting to analyze what happens to search when you execute catalog holdouts, e-mail holdouts, and display ad geo-targeted holdouts.

Many clever marketers observe what happens to search in holdout situations. Not surprisingly, search activity increases when marketing is increased, and search activity decreases when marketing spend is decreased --- independent of what you want to spend on search.

In other words, search is a leading indicator that other marketing activities are working.

It's been my experience that you have to attribute much of search spend back to other marketing activities. In other words, you don't evaluate search on the basis of what search generates, you evaluate search on the basis of how it helps improve conversion/response among other marketing activities.

Search orders, and search ad spend are attributed to other channels.

October 10

Ask an attribution expert to parse orders across the marketing activities that generated the order, and you'll have one happy attribution expert!

Ask the attribution expert to tell you what a customer will do in the future, once she successfully parses historical orders across marketing activities, and you'll see a blank stare emerge.

More than anything, this is what is wrong with our lust for marketing attribution. It doesn't tell us anything about what will happen. It only tells us about one of a nearly infinite number of possible historical outcomes.

October 11

Catalog marketers have history on their side, and history yields perspective. Perspective tells us that it is really important to know what will happen in the future.

Most of the larger catalog brands I work with are obsessed about their "file forecast".

The "file forecast" tells the catalog marketer what sales will look like in the next five years, given the strength of the customer file today.

Online/social/mobile marketers (and many attribution experts) have little idea what their initiatives will yield in the next five years, because their analysis tools are calibrated to measure "conversion".

If you run a traditional "file forecast", like old-school catalog marketers have been doing for more than thirty years, you'll quickly learn that some attribution activities are like "Fool's Gold". You'll quickly learn that parsing orders accurately yields very little improvement in the ability of a business to profitably grow a business over time.

October 12

Fear.

Read any marketing trade journal, and you'll see fear in action.

"Savvy marketers realize that in today's hostile business climate, an embrace of Social CRM is required to engage a disenchanted customer."

What exactly does that mean? If I don't engage a disenchanted customer, will I be out of business next year? Where's the proof?

The articles we read rarely provide proof. Instead, we're asked to blindly follow a fear-based argument that is strongly worded.

October 13

"If you're doing catalog copy online, you are dead".

Honestly, how prescient are folks these days? Do they have an ability to see six months ahead, noticing that if you are a catalog company and you, for whatever reason, place the same copy that exists in your catalog on your website, that you are going to be completely out of business? How do people know this?

This quote came from a vendor that has an interest in promoting unique and interesting copy in online channels.

Who is the author that wrote the quote? What is the author selling? That's what we need to look at as we attempt to navigate all of this marketing slush.

October 14

There should be tension between a marketer and a merchant.

You don't ever read about this in the blogosphere or on Twitter. Sure, you'll read all about the six easy steps that guarantee Christmas success (step #4 = make sure you have great product that customers love). The six easy tips are part of Marketing 101. The relationship between a marketer and a merchant, well, that's part of Marketing 801.

I'm not saying these two individuals should hate each other.

But there is a problem if these two individuals don't ever interact.

October 15

A solid merchant must own the merchandising strategy of every landing page, every e-mail campaign, every page in a catalog.

There's no way that a merchant is going to stand by and let a bunch of search marketers merchandise a landing page. There's no way that a merchant is going to let a bunch of web gurus merchandise an e-mail campaign.

The merchant cares deeply about her product, and is accountable for the sales of the item. The best merchants are going to demand that they make merchandising decisions.

October 16

A solid marketer must own the merchandising strategy of every landing page, every e-mail campaign, every page in catalog.

There's no way that a marketer is going to stand by and let a bunch of merchants determine what goes on a landing page. There's no way that a marketer is going to let a bunch of merchants merchandise an e-mail campaign.

The marketer cares deeply about the customer, and is accountable for the productivity of a customer. The best marketers are going to demand that they make merchandising decisions that are in the best interest of the customer.

October 17

When I worked at Lands' End (1990 – 1995), we had a monthly meeting where we reviewed the performance of the most recent catalog.

All key business leaders were invited to this meeting, especially the merchant leadership team.

Every catalog spread was posted on the conference room wall, backed by colored tag board.
- Gold = 30%+ Profit Rate.
- Green = 20% to 29% Profit Rate.
- Blue = 10% to 19% Profit Rate.
- Red = Less Than 10% Profit Rate.

If you want to make your merchandising team instantly accountable, this is how you do it.

Each spread was ordered in the room, so that pages 2-3 were on the far left, then pages 4-5, well, you get the picture.

Visually, the tag board "told a story". Everybody in the room knew that six red tag boards at the start of the catalog indicated a problem!

October 18

Of course, some of you believe that catalog marketing is so 1994.

Ok, fine.

You have landing pages. You have e-mail campaigns. You have tabs on your home page for every important merchandise division.

And maybe tag board is so 1994 as well. Ok, fine. Use technology to create one of those fabled "dashboards" that illustrates how profitable merchandise is on your website.

Just do something, please!

October 19

Do not take the easy way out here.

The easy way out is to illustrate conversion rates by key links on a page. You show that "x" percent of visitors clicked on the link, and "y" percent of the clickers converted with a purchase.

Easy.

A more interesting approach is to measure profit.

When you use click-through rates and conversion rates, you give the merchant an opportunity to blame you for a lack of performance. The merchant will tell you that it was your fault that customers didn't click on the merchandise.

By measuring profit, holistically, across your website, you put the accountability for merchandise productivity squarely upon the merchant.

October 20

This brings up an interesting topic.

Analytics experts like to focus on "attribution" models, trying to parse orders across the marketing activities that may have caused the order.

A better use of time is "on-site attribution". In other words, you parse visitor clicks to the items on the website, and then you measure the profitability of every item on the website. If certain items are featured on the home page, then those items are given a disproportionate amount of the marketing expense required to drive traffic to the home page.

This is a very different discipline … one you seldom if ever hear about. That should tell you that it is a discipline worth pursuing.

October 21

The concept isn't hard. Say, for the sake of simplicity, that you feature ten items on your home page. Say that you spend $10,000 driving traffic to the home page.

Every item that the customer sees is attributed a share of the $10,000 of marketing expense. Obviously, if an item is clicked, then marketing expense is attributed to the click. But if an item is viewed, then, yes, marketing expense is also attributed to the view.

Sum up all views and clicks, divide marketing expense against views and clicks, and the end result is a profit and loss statement for all items viewed and clicked.

Yes, this is important, you should be running this analysis against every item you sell, allocating marketing spend and website maintenance expenses against every item viewed, and every item clicked.

October 22

The magic of your website becomes apparent when you allocate clicks and views against marketing spend, and against website maintenance expenses.

A few things will pop out at you.
1. You'll immediately see that various items are "over-exposed".
2. You'll immediately see that various items are "under-exposed".

Immediately capitalize on the "under-exposed" items, feature them on all relevant landing pages, feature the best items on your home page.

Of course, what I'm explaining is very elementary.

But almost nobody is doing this.

An entire generation of web analysts have not been trained to conduct a proper merchandise analysis. And though it is important to do marketing analysis, all of the secrets of the business are in the analysis of merchandise productivity. Merchandise productivity is the lifeblood of a business.

October 23

The marketing expert must be proficient in merchandise analysis. It is the only way that the marketer can compete with the merchant.

While many readers would say that I'm not qualified to talk about marketing, that I'm only a "database marketer", I can say that I've worked in three billion-dollar-plus businesses for a total of eighteen years, and all of those years were spent working in the marketing department. So I've seen a few things happen in my time.

The merchant is going to needle the marketer, non-stop, until the merchant believes that the marketer has done every single thing possible to sell what the merchant is offering.

The merchant will say that your e-mail campaigns aren't "brand appropriate" or "don't tell a story".

The merchant will say that landing pages are poorly designed.

The merchant will say that your catalogs "aren't aspirational".

The merchant will say that the social media presence isn't yielding "viral opportunities".

The merchant will say that the mobile version of your website "doesn't bring the brand to life".

The marketer has to have facts, so that the marketer can level the playing surface.

October 24

The marketer has to have data to level the playing surface.

The marketer must be able to demonstrate that various product, placed on the home page and on landing pages, performed well below expectations. The marketer must then demonstrate that the merchant is accountable for any item that performs below expectations despite being offered prominent real estate.

October 25

In baseball, there is a metric called "VORP", or "Value Over Replacement Player" (http://en.wikipedia.org/wiki/Value_over_replacement_player).

If you first baseman was hurt, and you had to replace the first baseman with a bench player or somebody off the waiver wire, you know what it is you have lost, right? What you have lost is the "Value Over a Replacement Player."

Bad baseball teams win about 60 games.

Great baseball teams win about 100 games.

The difference, $100 - 60 = 40$, is the "Value" that each of eight starting position players and ten pitchers deliver, above and beyond a team of replacement players.

Why I am talking about baseball? Read on!

October 26

If "VORP" is a useful metric in baseball, then why can't "VORP" be a useful metric in e-commerce?

Instead of "Value Over Replacement Player", why not measure "Value Over Replacement Product"?

Now, I'd prefer to measure profit per visitor or profit per view/click, but let's keep things simple.

Pretend that an item on the home page generates $0.30 per view.

Now, pretend that you had to choose an item at random to replace the featured item. That item generates $0.20 per view.

The difference between $0.30 and $0.20 is, of course, $0.10.

$0.10 is the "Value Over Replacement Product".

October 27

If you have a million visitors to your website each year, and you know that an item has a $0.10 "VORP", or "Value Over Replacement Product", then that item provides 1,000,000 * $0.10 = $100,000 of incremental demand.

October 28

The marketer finally has a metric that can be used as part of a reasonable discussion with a merchant.

When the merchant complains that a specific item isn't being featured often enough on a valuable landing page, you can communicate that the item has a VORP of -$0.04, costing your business $40,000 demand for every 1,000,000 visitors.

October 29

If you're going to have "VORP", you better have "VORC", too.

"VORC", of course, is "Value Over Replacement Customer".

This metric is easy to understand, and works very well when considering customer service problems.

Say you have an average twelve-month buyer that is forecast to generate $18 profit in the next year.

Say you lose $12.00 profit acquiring a new customer, and then that customer generates $13 profit in the next twelve months.

Value Over Replacement Customer is $18 – ($13 + -$12) = $19.

In other words, your loyal customer has a VORC of $19 compared with the replacement value of a customer.

Loyalty consultants, of course, are going to love VORC, because it "proves" that it costs a lot more to acquire a new customer than to retain an existing customer.

October 30

If you are a marketer or an analytics expert, you are fully aware that communication is the most important tool you have.

Nobody is really interested in fancy metrics like VORP or VORC. Your co-workers are interested in stories, stories that resonate with their world view.

If you really want to test your marketing mettle, start an in-house blog that can only be read by employees. If you do a great job, your co-workers will subscribe to your blog. If your co-workers do not subscribe to your blog, well, you know you have a communication problem, don't you?

October 31

You want to know what I find to be scary?

Discounts and promotions.

Now, I have no problem with a business like Zappos, who builds the cost of free shipping into the cost of an item. Every customer is being treated the same way, every customer knows they are buying an item for $72 and it will be shipped really fast to their home.

I do have a problem with a business that charges $14.95 for shipping and handling to the core customer, then offers free shipping and 10% off your order to e-mail subscribers, and then suggests that e-mail marketing is relevant and interesting.

Obviously, there's the inherent unfairness involved in charging customers different prices for the same items and same service. And yes, I've been responsible for promotions in past lives … so I know about the competitive and overstocked item and internal pressures that result in a marketer offering a promotion.

More important, there's the internal pressure that is applied to the profit and loss statement.

Your garden-variety CFO views the world through a different set of glasses than you do. She likes to look at ratios, like marketing dollars as a percentage of net sales. She doesn't like to see this ratio get out of line, she knows that most marketers have a hard time tracking return on investment, so she's going to focus on this ratio (called the "ad-to-sales" ratio) as her way of keeping the marketing department in line.

So your garden-variety CFO is going to add all of your 10% off and free shipping expenses to the marketing line in your p&l statement. Even if your sales increase, your ad-to-sales ratio is likely to inflate. Once that ratio inflates, your CFO will demand that you cut spending somewhere. Those cuts can happen in paid search, or display ads, or offline marketing, or any of a number of places.

Or, the CFO can ask the company to start trimming headcount, so that corporate expense ratios are acceptable.

You might be all about optimization and testing and maximizing the return on investment of marketing activities, but your way of thinking doesn't align with the CFO. Your CFO is going to look at ratios, and is going to make sure that all ratios yield a satisfactory profit and loss statement.

Too often, I've been associated with businesses that start trimming headcount, cap salary increases, or reduce capital expenditures (in addition to cutting marketing spend) as ratios get out of line.

Discounts and promotions lead to short-term increases in sales. They are like the temporary benefit you get from drinking a bottle of Mountain Dew every day for a few months.

Down the road, discounts and promotions lead to a customer base that is less likely to purchase full-priced merchandise. Expense ratios get out of line. Budgets get cut, human beings are fired, employees don't get raises, capital expenditures are reduced. It's like putting the Mountain Dew fanatic on a diet because of a risk of diabetes.

You cannot see the long-term impact of drinking Mountain Dew when you are sitting in your recliner enjoying a single can of Mountain Dew ... you only get to enjoy the short-term benefit of the beverage.

Similarly, our web analytics solutions have a very hard time pointing out the long-term impact of discounts and promotions. A combination of short-term benefits and the inability to measure long-term effects are leading us toward a scary outcome.

November 1

Have you ever spent time reading blogs?

There are blogs supported by facts, and there are blogs built on opinions.

You are always better off focusing on content supported by facts.

This morning, I read a blog post from a marketing journalist. The marketing journalist was disappointed that a company discontinued their catalog marketing program. The marketing journalist called the decision "short sighted", then went on to further criticize the brand for not recognizing the importance of customer service.

A few questions for the marketing journalist:
1. Do you have access to a profit and loss statement that illustrates the effectiveness of the catalog marketing program?
2. Do you have access to consumer business intelligence that tells you what customers shopping this brand think of this marketing channel?
3. Do you have access to actual customer purchase transactions, so that you can see how customers truly behave?

In all likelihood, the marketing journalist doesn't have the facts. Instead, the marketing journalist has a set of opinions that are designed to help sell advertising space.

Always ask yourself what the author is selling.

November 2

Marketing is really different in 2011 than it was in 1991.

Back in 1991, the marketer was sort of a "Master".

In other words, the marketer had to be an expert at a lot of things. She had to be a financial expert, thoroughly understanding the profit and loss statement. She had to know how each marketing tactic contributed to short-term and long-term profitability. She had to know exactly how many customers she needed to acquire during the year, in order to grow the business to an acceptable level.

She had to convince the merchandising team that she needed various creative merchandise presentations in order to obtain success. She had to convince the call center that it was important to cross-sell or up-sell certain items, even offering bonuses and incentives to do this. She was a brilliant collaborator. She earned the trust of the CFO.

This "Master" doesn't seem to exist in 2011, or at least it is really hard to find a true "Digital Marketing Master".

Quick ... name three individuals who possess these skills across all Digital Marketing channels?

November 3

Last year, I spoke at a conference, and I offered the audience (2/3 were catalog marketers) a choice. If they had to cut one job from the marketing department, which job would they cut?

- Catalog Marketing Director with 20 years of experience.
- Online Marketing Director with 10 years of experience.
- Social Media Manager with 2 years of Social Media experience.

The audience overwhelming chose to vote the Catalog Marketing Director off of the island.

If you were CEO, which individual would you downsize, and why?

November 4

Back in 1991, experience mattered. You wanted to hire a "Master" who had a lot of experience, and possessed a breadth of knowledge across disciplines.

If you were an employee, you could identify a career path that yielded a position of significant responsibility. It wasn't easy to achieve your career dreams, because a ton of people were competing for the same position, but it was possible.

In 2011, what is the career path that leads to an individual being a marketing "Master"? Have you thought about this?

November 5

Which set of skills is most important when thinking about hiring a new Chief Marketing Officer? Rank order the following set of skills, in order of importance:

- Social Media.
- Mobile.
- Display Ads & Re-Targeting.
- E-Mail Marketing.
- Paid Search.

- Search Engine Optimization.
- Creative (i.e. photography & display of merchandise).
- Copywriting.
- Offline and Online Analytics.
- Catalog Marketing.
- Loyalty Marketing.
- Newspaper Advertising.
- Radio Advertising.
- Television Advertising.
- Billboard Advertising.
- Print Ads and Magazine Ads.
- Field Marketing.
- Public Relations.
- Multi-Channel Marketing.
- All Other Marketing Activities.

November 6

Which set of marketing channels yields the greatest return on investment, in your opinion? Rank order the following marketing channels, in order of return on investment.
- Social Media.
- Mobile.
- Display Ads & Re-Targeting.
- E-Mail Marketing.
- Paid Search.
- Search Engine Optimization.
- Creative (i.e. photography & display of merchandise).
- Copywriting.
- Offline and Online Analytics.
- Catalog Marketing.
- Loyalty Marketing.
- Newspaper Advertising.
- Radio Advertising.
- Television Advertising.
- Billboard Advertising.
- Print Ads and Magazine Ads.
- Field Marketing.
- Public Relations.
- Multi-Channel Marketing.
- All Other Marketing Activities.

November 7

Did the marketing channels that deliver the best return on investment align with the marketing channels that you'd value when looking for a Chief Marketing Officer?

If not, why not?

November 8

I'm going to guess that your rank-ordering of marketing channel knowledge needed by a Chief Marketing Officer is heavily skewed to newer marketing channels, right?

Odds are that you'd look for social and mobile and various online marketing expertise, and who could blame you, those are the channels that get all of the attention these days.

But are those the skills that are most important to your business?

Do those channels deliver the greatest return on investment?

Do the folks who possess those skills fit well within your corporate culture?

Our marketing disapora is in full force. What was once a homogenous group of leaders focused on a craft became a veritable plethora of micro-disciplines, represented by small tribes of passionate believers.

Somehow, we need to identify leaders, those who have the perspective necessary to understand not how channels fit together, but instead, have the perspective to understand how products, brands, channels, employees, and customers fit together.

I fear that this discipline is getting harder and harder to find.

November 9

Are you tired of your job?

In 2009, you were stuck. You couldn't leave your job, heck, folks were losing their jobs all around you. It was a minor miracle that you were able to keep your job!!

Now, we're at the end of 2011. And even though the job market is tough, there are jobs out there for qualified individuals.

The best time to create the environment for a successful job search is in the twelve months prior to a job search. You build your LinkedIn network in the year prior to a job change, you create your blog and demonstrate thought leadership in the year before a job change, you manage Facebook and Twitter in an appropriate manner in the year before a job change.

2009 was awful. I kept getting messages from folks who had just lost their job. They were looking for any angle possible to get a new job. They were forced to build their online network on-the-fly, they simply had no choice.

Do the opposite. Proactively build your online network, so that you are ready for any possible outcome!

November 10

Cyber Monday.

It's just eighteen days away. And if you read what the punditocracy has to say about Cyber Monday, you'd think this is the most important day in the history of mankind, or at least the most important day in the history of e-commerce.

Here's a little thought for you. If this day is so critically important, if there are so many customers out there looking to purchase something on this day and this day only, then why are you being asked to completely cheapen your brand by providing customers discounts and promotions on Cyber Monday?

Don't give me that lame "market share" argument. This is one day out of 365. Are we to believe that we'll lose out on a plethora of future business by not offering some special item at 50% off with free next-day shipping?

Quick, tell me which brands you purchased from on Cyber Monday, 2008?

Exactly.

November 11

Here's an analysis request for you.

Go back to 2010, and create two segments of customers.
1. Customers who purchased on Cyber Monday 2010.
2. Customers who purchased the day before, and the day after Cyber Monday 2010.

Measure annual repurchase rate, spend per retained buyer, and profit per customer in each segment.

Again, this isn't something you're going to easily answer in Google Analytics. You're going to have to do a little bit of heavy lifting.

But that's ok. You may find that Cyber Monday buyers are worth more than similar customers buying on either day around Cyber Monday, and if that is the case, then offer every possible discount and promotion under the sun on Cyber Monday.

Maybe you learn the opposite. Maybe you learn that all you did is build a customer file of promotional buyers who don't generate profit the rest of the year.

Either way, you'll know more about your business than you do by listening to the punditocracy.

November 12

If you employ a statistician, give her a fun job.
- Create 365 dummy variables, one for each day the customer purchased in 2009.
- Create RFM-based variables to control for customer quality.
- Based on the purchase day in 2009, run a regression model that uses the 365 dummy variables as independent variables. Let your dependent variable be profit per customer in 2010.

See where Cyber Monday stacks up as a day for generating profitable customers against every other day during the year.

I'll bet you learn something really interesting here!

November 13

Here's another Cyber Monday test.

Pull every customer who purchased because of a promotion in 2009, and then measure if Cyber Monday yielded a more profitable customer in 2010 than you get from running other promotions during the year.

November 14

When evaluating Cyber Monday, be certain to quantify the percentage of customers who are new to your brand.

If 88% of Cyber Monday buyers are existing customers, then you have a analytics challenge ahead of you. In that case, you have to demonstrate that the Cyber Monday purchase is an "incremental purchase", one that wouldn't have happened unless this blessed, promotion-laden event was unleashed upon e-commerce brands by the trade industry.

If 88% of your Cyber Monday buyers are first-time buyers, well, that's probably not a bad thing, assuming that discount/promo newbies convert to full-price buyers in the future.

November 15

Make sure you conduct a merchandise analysis of Cyber Monday.

In other words, make sure that you thoroughly understand the merchandise preference of the Cyber Monday buyer. If the merchandise preferred by the Cyber Monday buyer is different than the merchandise purchased by buyers during the rest of the Christmas season, you may have both a marketing opportunity and a long-term customer value challenge. Anytime you acquire customers who have a merchandise preference that is outside the average customer, you have a future value challenge awaiting you!

November 16

Be sure to segment Cyber Monday buyers that come from e-mail marketing, and analyze them as a separate segment among all Cyber Monday buyers.

Your e-mail list is often skewed to better customers who prefer discounts and promotions. You want to understand what fraction of your Cyber Monday sales is attributed to e-mail marketing, and you want to understand the fraction of Cyber Monday sales generated by all other marketing channels.

November 17

Compare Cyber Monday buyers purchasing in the e-commerce channel to Cyber Monday buyers who purchase via the telephone. Often, the telephone buyer is "old-school", and may not even be aware that Cyber Monday exists. When this happens, there are differences in long-term value.

November 18

Compare the percentage of future demand obtained via discounts and promotions for Cyber Monday buyers, for all other discount/promo buyers, and for full-price buyers. Are these customers trained to purchase via discounts/promos, or are these customers amenable to full-price purchases in the future?

November 19

If you have a retail channel, it is great fun to compare the Cyber Monday buyer to the Black Friday buyer.

Both customers share the zeal of "getting a deal".

The Black Friday customer is a more social, event driven customer looking for immediate gratification.

The Cyber Monday buyer has the patience to wait out the weekend and has the patience to wait up to a week to receive merchandise.

Both make for great segmentation variables.

November 20

In fact, for the remainder of the Christmas season, create segmentation variables for Cyber Monday buyers and Black Friday buyers.

Do these customers ever visit your website again? If they do, that's a good thing!

November 21

Oh, this is such a fun time of the year. And it starts today, the week of Thanksgiving!

There are three things that are fun about this time of year.
1. The festive excitement of Thanksgiving/Christmas/New Year's Day.
2. The final three weeks of e-commerce sales before the end of the year.
3. All of the days off you'll get between now and December 31.

Your Executive team doesn't think the final three weeks of sales before Christmas is fun. For many business leaders, bonus potential is either realized or squandered during these three weeks!

In some ways, the die is cast. You've planned for these three weeks for the better part of a year. Most of what happens next is out of your control.

Try to take a deep breath of fresh air this week.

November 22

If you're a retailer, this is a good time to call your best customers and invite them to your store for a special Black Friday event.

Most retailers try to open early (i.e. 4:30am) to capture the attention of the audience, coupled with some whopper of a promotion on a handful of items with limited availability.

Why not do something different, especially with your best customers?

Just don't call it a "doorbuster". Remember the poor woman who died a few years ago when customers actually broke down the door at a Wal-Mart? Marketers sometimes fail to grasp the concept of accountability ... we work the public into a frenzy, then we stand far away when our promotions cause the loss of a life.

Why not do something different this year?

November 23

Your customer knows she is going to receive big discounts on promoted items this Friday, in-store.

Your customer knows she is going to receive free shipping and a percentage off and savings on key items on Cyber Monday.

So ask yourself why a customer would purchase from your brand today, the day before Thanksgiving? This customer behaves different from those the press will lather themselves over in a few days. It might be a good idea to find out what motivates this customer.

November 24

Happy Thanksgiving!

No work today, ok?

November 25

Black Friday.

By now, you're read the predictions.
- Black Friday sales are forecast to increase by 5.3%.
- Black Friday sales are forecast to increase by 3.6%.
- Black Friday sales are forecast to increase by 1.8%.
- Those offering big discounts and promotions will be the big winners.

Nobody goes back and verifies that the predictions were accurate. Nope, it's all part of a big show designed to generate interest in retailing.

Quick, tell me the stores you purchased from and the items you bought and the amount you saved on Black Friday 2009?

Yup, that's how memorable this event is.

I think you're better served to create an event during some other time of the year, an event where you aren't competing with everybody else on a race to the bottom of the pricing ladder, an event that actually causes a customer to feel good, to feel special.

November 26

If you are a retailer, go back and measure the relationship between Black Friday comp store sales, and comp store sales from the day after Black Friday through Christmas.

Is there a relationship?

If there isn't a relationship, don't feel too bad if yesterday didn't meet expectations, with the exception of the sales you believe you lost yesterday.

November 27

There are the trade organizations that created and promote Cyber Monday.

Then there are the consulting firms, bloggers, research organizations, and trade organizations that know that customers spend more on each subsequent Monday that customers spend on Cyber Monday. These organizations are going to ram their research down your throat in an effort to drown out Cyber Monday. They'll be right, and nobody will care.

None of it matters. Who cares that Cyber Monday will be a trending topic on Twitter? When is the last time you profited because of a trending topic on Twitter?

All that matters is what you sell, when you sell it, the customers you serve, and how much profit you generate by selling something.

November 28

Happy Cyber Monday!

Since you feel compelled to participate, do a nice job of providing real-time analytics of the event. Measure East Coast sales in the morning, and see if you can project West Coast sales based on what you're seeing. Carefully track if customers are shifting orders earlier in the day. Track "Cyber Monday" sentiment via social media, comparing this year to last year. Track the key items your competition chose to give away in their promotions. Have a small holdout sample that did not receive any of your promotions, and compare their spend to customers who you happily gave precious gross margin dollars to.

Accumulate business intelligence today, and report on your findings this evening, so that Management knows first thing tomorrow morning how this event impacted your business.

And that's all I'm going to say about Cyber Monday.

November 29

Business leaders plan ahead for 2012. So if you've been focused on other things, use this week to craft your vision for 2012.

This means you identify the most important goals and objectives, prioritizing what is likely to deliver the best return on investment in 2012. This means writing objectives for your direct reports. This means communicating your vision to co-workers, your leadership team, and your direct reports.

You want to nail this part of the 2012 planning process, so that your employees know exactly what they are going to work on when the new year begins.

November 30

If you are a catalog marketer, you've probably set up a series of in-home tests, designed to determine the optimal dates to contact customers during the latter portion of the Christmas shopping season.

Always test how late you can profitably generate sales.

Always test how few pages it takes to profitably generate sales.

December 1

We begin December by evaluating the hot topics in e-commerce and multi-channel marketing. After all, you're spending time in December crafting your strategy for 2012, so why don't we review where various disciplines are heading?

December 2

Let's start with an old-school channel, namely, catalog marketing.

Catalog marketing faces a decade of reckoning. More than any other marketing channel, catalog marketing rode the wave of demographics to amazing heights in the five decades after World War II. Now, catalog marketing is riding the Baby Boomer generation into niche status.

When you analyze the demographics of the catalog marketing shopper, you continually observe an audience that is approaching sixty years of age. In other words, the catalog marketing generation is largely the Baby Boomer generation.

In the next ten years, the Baby Boomer generation will begin to retire in large numbers. It is doubtful that twenty-five year old customers will adopt catalog marketing in numbers sufficient to replace customers being lost by retirement.

We are going to see a significant transformation among catalog brands. Some catalog brands will enjoy a golden era, as the Baby Boomer generation moves into their demographic. Some catalog brands will successfully transition into niche brands serving an older demographic in rural areas. Some catalog brands will successfully transition into the e-commerce channel, generating sales via e-commerce instead of using catalogs to drive customers into the e-commerce channel.

And some catalog brands will simply die off, in a slow and painful way.

Baby Boomers will be between 47 and 67 years old in 2012. The core catalog shopping population is going to retire in large numbers in the next ten years. This will signal the end of a generational wave of marketing success. There will be huge profit opportunities available for marketers who manage this transition effectively.

December 3

The e-mail marketer is under assault.

We just talked about catalog marketing, a discipline that will be torn apart by demographics over the next decade.

E-mail is a marketing channel that is being torn apart by technology, not demographics.

We intuitively know that social media is fundamentally better at facilitating conversations that e-mail marketing is, if it weren't better, then we wouldn't see between a half-billion and a billion folks worldwide using social media.

This creates significant opportunities for the e-mail marketer. In the 2000s, we treated e-mail as a mass-marketing opportunity. We grew a giant list of subscribers, and if lucky, we had the resources to create a few versions of an e-mail campaign that were sent to segmented audiences. We generated $0.20 sales per recipient, which yielded $0.07 profit. We summed a ton of small numbers, yielding large amounts of profit!

I repeatedly run into marketing leaders who lament declining open rates, click-through rates, and conversion rates.

Don't lament your metrics, embrace them!

What we are seeing is the "erosion of the unengaged", if you will. In other words, two-thirds of the e-mail marketing list never really cared about your campaigns. They passively signed up for your e-mail marketing campaigns, or were forced to sign up by your purchase process, so they never really cared in the first place about what you were doing.

As social media consumes the marginal portion of the e-mail customer file, we'll continue to witness reduced open, click, and conversion rates. This will cause the e-mail marketer to embrace the small portion of the e-mail file that continues to generate business.

Maybe you have an e-mail marketing list of 100,000 subscribers, a list that took you a decade to build. In the next decade, this list of 100,000 subscribers will become a list of 10,000 who adore e-mail marketing, while the remaining 90,000 will slowly leak out into other channels, like social media and mobile.

I think the best e-mail marketers already recognize this. I think the best e-mail marketers know they need to really focus on the best 10% of the e-mail list. I think the best e-mail marketers aren't worrying about declining rates in the bottom 90% of the e-mail marketing list, because those were e-mail addresses that never really mattered in the first place.

This is a version of "channel evolution" that is perfectly acceptable. Catalog marketers went through this in the 2000s. E-mail marketers will go through this in the 2010s. Embrace change, don't fight it!

December 4

I've always had a soft spot for search. According to Google, I search for content 1,200 times a year, somewhere between three and four times a day.

That being said, something is up in search.

Three years ago, Google was responsible for fifty percent of the traffic to my blog. In late 2010, Twitter was responsible for fifty percent of the traffic to my blog, with Google only driving a quarter of the traffic. By the time you read this, in late 2011, the trend should be even more exaggerated.

When the world wide web exploded, we needed a way to find the information we were looking for. Search filled that need, in a spectacular way.

Now Facebook, Twitter and social media in general are muscling in.

I'm not smart enough to know how search responds to this shift in user behavior.

And I'm not smart enough to know how businesses will respond to changes in search.

I am smart enough to know that all marketing channels that are fueled by technology "peak". Technology-based marketing channels rise to prominence, are then challenged by new technology, then find a niche and thrive or slowly die off.

E-commerce folks will undoubtedly find that a portion of the customer file will always use and like search. This will lead to advanced segmentation techniques that leverage unique customer behaviors. We are going to spend more time analyzing and understanding the evolutionary behavior of a customer who used to adore search, and we'll make better investments in marketing as a result.

Again, I'm not smart enough to know how technology-fueled marketing channels will evolve. I am smart enough to know that all channels "peak", and after a channel peaks, there are amazing opportunities to generate profit. Catalog marketing and e-mail marketing are two examples of channels that peaked, and are now generating significant profit opportunities to marketers who capitalize on those channels within the niche that appreciates catalogs and e-mail campaigns.

December 5

Social Media.

It's unlikely we've ever seen a marketing channel that received this much hype, and generated so little incremental sales.

This isn't the fault of social media. This is our fault, for believing the hype. Social media, in and of itself, never promised us anything.

And when we attempt social media activities and we fail, it isn't necessarily our fault, either. So much of what happens in this realm is outside of our control, in fact, almost everything in this realm is outside of our control.

I like to compare six list sizes.
- The number of customers purchasing in the past twelve months (300,000).
- The number of e-mail subscribers I have (220,000).
- The number of individuals clicking through an e-mail campaign, past twelve months (31,000).
- The number of individuals buying from an e-mail campaign, past twelve months (13,000).
- The number of unique Facebook/Twitter Fans/Followers I have (13,000).
- The number of Facebook/Twitter customers purchasing at least one time in the past year because of social media (1,200).

This always helps me understand the place that social media plays in the evolution of my business. For 95 of 100 e-commerce businesses, we learn that social media plays a tiny role in generating sales, but plays a significant role in the communication patters of our customers.

That's the mystery of social media. Everybody is using it, almost nobody is purchasing merchandise because of it!

I'm not hopeful that this is going to change in 2012. Social media, in some ways, is like a telephone was in the 1980s ... everybody used a telephone, but that didn't mean that everybody was responsive to telemarketing.

And if there's one thing we know about technology, it is that there is always something that replaces what previously dominated the marketplace. In Social media, this is particularly worrisome. We went from AOL's "You've Got Mail" to Geocities to MySpace to Blogs to Second Life to Facebook to Twitter to Foresquare.

In other words, it is entirely possible that something replaces Facebook and Twitter in the next few years.

We spent the 2000s building our online presence, crafting e-commerce websites and growing our online marketing presence.

We've spent the past five years responding to a changing marketplace by getting in bed with Google, Facebook, and Twitter. They control and direct traffic, we simply beg to be part of the process. We've slowly given a chunk of our brand equity to the traffic police. When those entities lose out, and the evolution of technology demonstrates that these entities will probably lose out over time, we lose the chunk of brand equity we gave them.

I'm convinced we will always have to participate in social media. I am not convinced that we'll ever see social media account for more than a small percentage of annual sales, maybe 5% to 10% of total e-commerce sales, with a small fraction of brands achieving significantly higher percentages. Increasingly, I believe that there will be something in the next five years that is far better than social media, I call it "Hologram Marketing". This will replace e-commerce, social, and mobile.

December 6

Mobile is an interesting channel.

I don't think any of us are smart enough to know where mobile is heading, we can just tell that it is going to have commerce potential that far exceeds social media.

You look at eBay, generating more than a billion in mobile sales … that tells you something. You never witnessed that kind of sales potential out of social media.

Of course, the sales at eBay aren't incremental sales, instead, mobile is cannibalizing sales previously generated by the e-commerce channel.

Mobile is different than e-commerce. Fifteen years ago, it was self-evident that e-commerce was going to be a huge sales channel. Today, it is self-evident that mobile is going to be a huge channel.

Notice that I left the word "sales" out of the last sentence!

For some of us, mobile will become a significant portion of sales, especially for businesses that have a "real-time" component. Retailers are very likely to benefit from mobile, as the mobile channel can provide real-time information.

For some of us, mobile will be a customer service channel. In B2B marketing, the sales person visiting a client can have instant access to unlimited information via mobile. You can see mobile replacing the catalog that a sales person used to bring on a client visit, right?

For many of us, mobile will be just another in a long line of channels that contribute "nickels and dimes". For many of us, we'll get a nickel from social, a nickel from mobile, a nickel from search, a nickel from e-mail marketing, you get the picture.

Longer-term, mobile fits into my vision of "Hologram Marketing". Your hand-held device will project an image that you interact with, an image that answers all of your questions and connects you with your network of friends. The hologram replaces your iPod, your iPad, your GPS, your mobile phone, your need for Google-based Search, Facebook, Twitter, Foresquare, basically everything. Hologram Marketing takes local in amazing directions.

December 7

Multi-Channel Marketing.

I'm not sure where this movement is heading.

You never hear the social/mobile folks talk about being "multi-channel". You never heard the e-commerce folks talk about it until mobile burst on to the scene.

Rather, "multi-channel" appears to be an argument that is offered by those loyal to an older technology. Multi-channel provides a bridge between the past and a vision of the future promoted by those using older technology.

Instead of thinking "multi-channel", we're better off thinking "transition", as in "how do we transition our customers from old to new?" Or "should we transition our customers from old to new?"

It's almost a given that we have to play in many different venues. This doesn't mean that our customers like to shop this way, and this doesn't mean that the future requires us to "be everywhere".

Apple isn't everywhere. Zappos isn't everywhere. Amazon isn't everywhere. Sometimes, you do things so well that your customers pull you into their world. You don't have to be offline and online and in retail stores and in all new technologies. You simply have to do what is right for your customer.

December 8

Old-school marketing.

You constantly read about the "death" of various marketing channels.

Let me ask you a pair of questions.
- Have you thrown out all the televisions in your home, because online video is so much more robust than television?
- Did you rip the radio out of your car because your iPod provides a better entertainment experience?

In other words, old-school marketing channels are not dead, they aren't irrelevant, they aren't unimportant.

In fact, if you take a look at the top twenty brands on Facebook, the brands that have the most "fans", you'll see a veritable plethora of old-school brands that leverage old-school marketing.

Do what is right for your customer. Always do what is right for your customer.

December 9

Copy.

I actively wonder what the future of copywriting is. After all, we've outsourced all of the good aspects of copywriting to our customers. Our customers write reviews of product, and our customers appear to trust what other customers write.

Nobody seems to trust what a copywriter has to say.

We did copywriters a disservice in the past decade. As social media surged, we asked our copywriters to focus on boring details. The copywriter tells us that a product is 8" x 12" x 2", the customer tells us that the unit runs at a 110 degree temperature, requiring adequate ventilation! We hire a social media guru to connect with customers on a blog, while we ask the copywriter to plug in eight important keywords that improve search engine optimization opportunities ... the customer writes for other customers, the copywriter writes for Google.

If I were a copywriter, I'd be planning a revolt of some sort in 2012. An entire profession/discipline is imploding.

December 10

We talked earlier about the marketing "Master", how this person doesn't seem to exist anymore.

2012 may represent the year when a marketing "Master" re-emerges. We'll be a decade into the social media era, we'll be five years into mobile, we'll be nearly twenty years into the evolution of e-commerce. That's enough time for somebody to emerge with the skills necessary to know how everything fits together.

Maybe it's better to say that the "Master" understands the customer. When you understand the customer, everything else falls into place.

At some point, and it may as well be 2012, somebody is going to gain enough business intelligence about customer behavior to enable a marketing "Master" to grow sales at an acceptable rate. Channels will not be the key, understanding the customer will be the key!

December 11

Understanding the customer.

We've spent a decade perfecting analytics tools that "understand campaigns". When we seek to optimize campaigns, we fail to optimize customers.

In 2012, the business intelligence community and the web analytics community have to answer a fundamental question.
- "Do we want to analyze campaigns, or do we want to analyze customers?"

As long as we continue to choose campaigns over customers, we will continue to push a cold, emotionless e-commerce reality fueled by keywords and referring URLs and discounts and promotions and Facebook campaigns and efforts to make videos go "viral".

In 2012, a small group of analytics experts will stand up, and take a different direction. This small group of analytics experts will provide a holistic view of customer behavior, across all channels. This small group of analytics experts will demonstrate that customers spend $300 a year, and that all other things we do add $50 a year, yielding a $350 customer. We'll understand that our customers have a base level of "brand loyalty", and we'll understand that all the other stuff is "frosting" that does cause an incremental increase in customer spend, but not the increase we think we're achieving.

December 12

When evaluating customer behavior, channels will become less relevant.

As you know, I spend a lot of time creating "Digital Profiles" for my clients. These are segments of customers that have comparable channel preferences and merchandise preferences.

These projects continue to illustrate a unique truth about customer behavior.
- Channels are much less relevant than we've been led to believe.
- Merchandise preference is much more important than we've been led to believe.

So many of these projects show that there aren't dramatic differences between search customers and e-mail customers and catalog shoppers. Rather, there are big differences between customers who buy from different merchandise divisions, a fact that enables us to utilize different channels to communicate different messages.

December 13

In 2012, we're likely to see a departure in marketing methodology.

We're always told that we have to have a consistent brand experience across all channels. We have to offer the same discounts and promotions in all channels. We have to offer the same merchandise in all channels. We have to offer the same type of customer service in all channels. We have to integrate all of our campaigns to take advantage of a customer who demands a consistent brand experience.

Every time we attempt to integrate all of our activities, we homogenize the customer experience.

I always wonder if my Digital Profile projects suggest little difference in customer behavior across channels because we, as marketers, have stripped out all of the unique benefits from each channel?

In 2012, we're likely to see a small group of marketers move in a different direction. This group of innovators will realize that it is ok for the mobile experience to be unique, to be catered to the unique interests of the mobile customer. This group of innovators will realize that the communication style used in social media must be different than in e-mail marketing or in catalog marketing, in order to be effective.

Heck, maybe the reason social media doesn't generate sales is because the message is homogenized and consistent with the message in other channels?

Somebody is going to figure out how to create a unique communication strategy within each channel to leverage the benefits of each channel. The days of the same message across all channels to best customers is winding down.

December 14

Leadership is likely to change in 2012.

It's really amazing to me that we're told we have to have the same marketing message across all channels to the same customer.

But in our companies, we organize differently, don't we?

We don't execute holistic projects. The CEO has a business question. The CEO asks the CMO (Chief Marketing Officer) to answer the question. The CMO looks to existing reporting for an answer, doesn't find it, then asks the web analytics expert, an information technology wizard, and a business intelligence expert separate questions, based on the unique abilities of each individual to answer a question.

Each party delivers a portion of the answer. The CMO cobbles the information together, and provides an answer for the CEO. The CEO has subsequent questions that are not answered by the CMO, so the CEO independently asks the web analytics expert, the information technology wizard, and the business intelligence expert to answer a different set of questions.

Answers to this second round of questions are sent to the CEO, who cobbles together original answers from the CMO with new answers from individual analytics experts, gets an answer that is 62% of what the CEO wanted, and then moves on.

This process repeats over and over and over. Nobody gets to see a holistic view of customer behavior.

In 2012, a small group of business leaders are going to become better at figuring out how to obtain accurate answers to customer intelligence questions across staffers with unique skill-sets. The questions will be more holistic in nature, with teams of individuals solving problems and all gaining an understanding of the business issue at the same time. This can only benefit the businesses we work for!

December 15

I've always wondered how a catalog, mailed to customers who never asked to receive a catalog can achieve a 4% or 5% response rate, while a website, which is being visited by customers with a clear and specific need that caused the visit to happen, only achieve a 4% or 5% conversion rate?

Think about it, folks.

When you look at how a catalog is put together, you see the vision of the merchant in action. The merchandising team is integrally involved in every single spread in the catalog.

When you look at how a website is put together, well, you sure don't see the impact of the merchant, do you? You see a combination of technology and landing pages optimized for a relationship with Google and a home page that is simultaneously owned by Corporate Marketing and Merchandising and Creative and the Online Marketing team, optimized by A/B tests that may or may not be relevant to the success of the business.

2012 has to be the year of the Merchant. The cold, sterile, technology-focused world of e-commerce needs the beneficial oversight provided by a merchant leader.

December 16

In fact, over the past fifteen years, the role of the Merchant has been in steady decline.

In the early days of e-commerce, this happened because the merchant didn't know how to write computer code, only information technology experts could write the code necessary to make a website look reasonable.

In the middle ages of e-commerce, everything on the site had to be optimal for the search engines. You didn't want a merchant messing with anything, because Google might get mad! Couple that with a set of "best practices" for putting the optimal assortment on the home page or landing pages, and it was "hands off" for the merchant team.

The last four years of social media madness further removed the merchant from the equation. It is no longer about product, now, the merchant must "join the conversation". Never mind that customers buy merchandise, the marketing world gave the impression that the customer won't buy merchandise unless the merchant has a genuine and authentic conversation with the customer.

The merchant is the cake, the marketer is the frosting. As you know, cake tastes better and better as you add frosting, until you get to a point where there is too much frosting.

We're at that point. Social media and mobile pushed us too far.

I have to believe that in 2012, the merchant is going to demand more cake and less frosting.

Just take a look at the number of Facebook Fans your business has in relationship to your e-mail marketing list, or in relationship to the number of twelve month buyers you have. For most of us, Facebook Fans are less than 10% of our twelve month buyer file ... focus on Facebook, and you take your eye off of the other 90% of the customer file. That doesn't sound like such a good idea!

December 17

Obviously, we're going to see more and more of what I call "experimental business models" in 2012. The Gilt / Woot / Groupon style of business model certainly opened eyes over the past few years. With organic growth becoming harder and harder to achieve, expect more unique and interesting business models.

The key, of course, is to understand your customer. If you are Neiman Marcus, your customer might not find much value in discounted merchandise. If you are Eddie Bauer, well, that might be a whole different thing, especially when you consider that a brand like Eddie Bauer has an Outlet division.

Experimentation is an important trend to follow in 2012. So much of e-commerce is cold, sterile, formatted, and algorithmic, requiring the creativity necessary to generate interest in merchandise.

December 18

If you are struggling with how to make investment decisions with unknown data, give the "square root rule" a try.

For example, say you spend $10,000 on paid search, and you generate $30,000 demand on that investment. Your CFO wants to know what would happen if you invested $20,000 in the paid search channel --- what kind of demand could you generate?

Use the following equation:
- Demand = (Old Demand) * ((New Investment / Old Investment) ^ 0.5).

In our example, here's what we get:
- Demand = ($30,000) * (($20,000 / $10,000) ^ 0.5).
- Demand = ($30,000) * (2^0.5).
- Demand = ($30,000) * (1.414).
- Demand = $42,420.

The equation works really well when you don't have good information to make decisions!

December 19

Your e-commerce business is really winding down now. There's maybe a day or two of expedited shipping orders coming, but for the most part, the full-price portion of the year is over.

Over the next three weeks, prepare your post-mortem of 2011.

Many companies employ a "post-mortem" process, comparing campaign effectiveness this year vs. last year vs. two years ago.

So often, this post mortem process is all about numbers, metrics, "KPIs" as folks like to say. Each business manager tells their own story ... e-mail worked, search worked, catalog worked, affiliates worked, website optimization worked, offline marketing worked, and oh, by the way, total sales increased by 1.1%.

Honestly, the post mortem process has to be all about "the story". Somebody has to tell a story about how customers behaved, in aggregate, over the past three years. Somebody has to explain how every single marketing activity worked, but the total business increased by only 1.1%.

I run into this problem repeatedly. A post mortem process used to uncover problems, because there were so few marketing activities that the focus was entirely on merchandise productivity. Today, there are so many marketing activities that it's hard to decompose why things worked, and why things didn't work.

I mentioned this earlier ... we need to shift our focus away from attributing orders to the marketing activities that allegedly caused the order to happen. We need to focus on understanding why customers spend more or less. We continue to focus on frosting, at a time when we need to focus on cake!

December 20

In the next week, we're going to focus on "encouragement". We're going to take a look at the positives of being in direct marketing during such fascinating times!

December 21

Catalog marketers are in desperate need of encouragement.

In spite of what nearly everybody says, catalog marketing still works! There are very few disciplines where you can send a customer an unwanted marketing material and generate a four percent response rate. The only way that happens is if customers truly want to receive your content.

Catalog marketing gives the merchant the most viable way to present merchandise in a creative and cohesive manner. You can't do this in an e-mail campaign, you can't do it online when the customer can bounce around from item to item, rendering storytelling feckless. Only with the catalog can you go from spread to spread, telling a cohesive story (though iPad apps have the potential to do this).

There is a subset of the population that loves catalog marketing. Focus your efforts on making this subset of the population happy! Take full advantage of the fact that catalog marketing is still the primary direct-to-consumer shopping channel for customers over the age of sixty.

Ignore what the pundits say. The pundits don't manage catalog marketing campaigns, they only pick on things they don't understand! Catalog marketing will never be what it was in the early 1990s, when it rode the rise of the Baby Boomer generation to new heights. But it will continue to be an effective marketing channel for the next decade among a 60+ audience that spent a lifetime loving this marketing channel.

December 22

E-mail marketers need to rise up and demand some love!

I frequently analyze the profitability of all marketing activities for direct marketers. A surprisingly small number of e-mail marketers stand up and demand love.

This is a story that isn't uncommon:
- Catalog Marketing
  - Annual Demand = $30,000,000. Ad Spend = $10,000,000. Profit = $2,000,000.
- E-Mail Marketing
  - Annual Demand = $8,000,000. Ad Spend = $300,000. Profit = $2,900,000.
- Paid Search
  - Annual Demand = $8,000,000. Ad Spend = $3,000,000. Profit = $200,000.
- Social Media
  - Annual Demand = $250,000. Ad Spend = $70,000. Profit = $5,000.
- Mobile
  - Annual demand = $200,000. Ad Spend = $100,000. Profit (Loss) = ($20,000).

You review the numbers, and two things stand out.
1. Social Media, oh boy.
2. E-Mail marketing really works!

The sin of e-mail marketing is that, in my example above, $2,900,000 profit is generated $0.07 at a time, so nobody ever notices what is really happening. Everybody talks about social media and engaged customers and all that good stuff, and for good reason. But nobody really talks about e-mail marketing, in total, and that's a shame.

E-mail marketers, stand up and demand to be counted! Run a profit and loss statement, and shout the results of an annual profit and loss statement to the Heavens!!

You matter!

You are not spammers.

You do not need to prove that your content is "relevant".

Show everybody the money!!!!!

December 23

I've yet to visit a company where the paid search manager receives the respect that is deserved.

As I understand it, the objective of the paid search manager is to link customers with specific problems or wants to the merchandise offered by a company that solves a problem or eliminates a want. That's a noble objective.

Within a company, here's what the merchant hears, when listening to any discussion about paid search:
- Keywords, bidding, optimization, branded, non-branded, long-tail, Google, Google, Google, Google, Google, Google, Bing.

It's hard for a merchant to get passionate about the long-tail of keywords.

The paid search manager has to be encouraged to speak a different language.

Turn paid search into a series of twelve marketing campaigns, one per month. Report on the merchandise that was sold, heck, present the merchandise from best-selling to most marginal in a Powerpoint presentation, or make it look like you are presenting results in a catalog format (i.e. spreads). Use a communication style that resonates with your merchandising team. Make your merchandising team crave paid search, help them appreciate the value of paid search.

You can do this! Speak the language of those who benefit from your efforts.

December 24

Are you responsible for social media at your company?

Holy cow, is this a tough job or what?

Earlier this year, an Executive told me something that is loosely paraphrased below:

- "Those social media folks get to play over there in fun-time land. I am accountable for generating sales, or I lose my job. They tweet pithy comments and have all sorts of meaningless conversations. I want them to be held accountable for generating revenue."

Back in 1996, I worked at Eddie Bauer, in the marketing department. I clearly recall the VP of Marketing stopping by and mocking our Manager of E-Commerce. He chided the individual for missing the sales forecast by 14%, because we only generated six e-commerce orders instead of the forecast of seven e-commerce orders! He couldn't believe that he had to staff an e-commerce division that was basically not generating anything of value.

Fifteen years later, can you deny that e-commerce is the best thing to happen to direct marketing in more than a hundred years?

It may be that social media is headed for a similar destination, we simply don't know.

What we do know is that a small number of over-zealous social media advocates have ruined it for everybody. A small number of individuals over-stated the benefits of social media, tainting the viewpoint of business leaders responsible for generating the profit that funds social media initiatives.

Be honest, how many times in history did something like Facebook go from zero to a half-billion or a billion users in a half-decade? Clearly, something is going on here!

Like any new kid on the block, the social media manager is going to have to build relationships. Yes, the social media manager is going to have to "join the conversation" within a company, with long-term employees who feel slighted that they are responsible for generating the profit that allows the social media manager the opportunity to engage with the customer base.

Use language and metrics that other people understand. Your CFO knows what incremental sales are all about (sales generated above and beyond all existing marketing activities), so communicate to your CFO using incremental sales estimates. If your customer spends $200 a year, and you think Facebook increases customer value by $5, then don't shy away from the fact that you have 50,000 Facebook Fans at $5 a year, yielding $250,000 of incremental sales.

Honestly, is there anything wrong with one employee generating $250,000 of incremental sales a year? Subtract cost of goods and pick/pack/ship expense, toss out annual salary and benefits, and the one social media employee is generating profit for the company.

Be willing to tell everybody that you are generating profit, don't hide behind industry buzzwords! It is very likely you are positively contributing to your brand, so make that clear to everybody who bothers to question your existence.

You can do this! Join the in-house conversation with your co-workers!

December 25

Merry Christmas! It certainly is a day to celebrate.

If you are an e-commerce business leader, it is a time to celebrate as well.

In spite of all of the challenges associated with e-commerce, your channel went from zero to mega-channel in just fifteen years. E-commerce grew when most channels struggled during The Great Recession.

E-commerce isn't popular anymore. The online world decided that it was a lot more fun to pontificate about social media and mobile than it was to talk about improving the shopping cart experience.

The e-commerce business leader is suffering the same fate that catalogers experienced when e-commerce blew catalog marketing out of the water. A decade ago, the catalog marketer was responsible for generating most of the business on an e-commerce website, but the e-commerce business leader got the credit for any business generated online. The e-commerce business leader received promotions, got salary increases, was invited to speak at conferences.

Today ... not so much.

Today, we'd rather hear about somebody who generated $100,000 on Facebook when the back-end infrastructure responsible for generating Facebook sales is managed by the e-commerce team.

Today, we'd rather talk about a mobile app that 2,198 customers downloaded, a mobile app that generated $40,000 of annual sales using the back-end infrastructure created by and managed by the e-commerce team.

Today, e-commerce simply "is". E-commerce business leaders are responsible for an undeniable decade of business improvements and incremental sales.

Be proud of what you've accomplished!

Without what you've accomplished, it would be really hard for social media experts and mobile advocates to be successful.

December 26

If you are lucky enough to be working in the mobile marketing industry, you probably already feel appreciated!

You probably feel a bit of pressure, too. So many folks are placing the mantle of sales growth upon you, at a time when we have no idea whether your channel will be a customer service channel or a legitimate sales driver. Sure, we believe the channel will be a legitimate sales driver, but we thought the same about social media, and for 95 out of 100 companies, that hasn't come true yet.

You are doing important work. Keep your head down. Don't listen to the outrageous expectations offered by the experts. Always demonstrate the sales you generated incrementally, and always demonstrate the sales that your channel "facilitated".

The work you are doing today is going to save many jobs in three to five years, as customer behavior evolves and changes. Hang in there! Take a rest when you need one, your job doesn't have to be a 24x7x365 endeavor. Be proud of your efforts, as it is likely that you are helping build our future!

December 27

Are you a CMO (Chief Marketing Officer)?

My goodness, that's not a fun job anymore. The pundits say that the average CMO tenure is something like two years.

You have a CFO who doesn't believe that your efforts generate a return on investment. You have an industry that says you aren't moving fast enough on social media and mobile. You have customers who have completely unreasonable expectations, customers who will publicly criticize your e-mail marketing efforts as "spam" to their loyal following of 98 followers. You have employees who will label your e-mail marketing efforts as "spam" because you didn't send them a relevant message.

A merchant is scrutinized for sourcing merchandise that doesn't sell. The metrics are so easy to understand, too ... either the item sold, or the item didn't sell, it's that simple!

The CMO doesn't have it so good. How the heck do you prove that a Facebook Fan yielded $8.34 of incremental demand? Nobody believes the geeky statistician who derived the estimate, everybody thinks that the math wizard simply manipulated numbers to tell whatever story the CMO wanted told.

I'd encourage you, the CMO under siege, to take your show on the road. You have a responsibility to teach every single employee how customers behave in 2012, illustrating how complex that behavior is compared to the behavior exhibited in 1997. Show them how little data you have to generate a relevant e-mail marketing message.

Even better, I encourage you to challenge your CFO or merchandising team to "do the job better". Let the CFO run the e-mail program for a month, let the CFO choose the creative and pick the merchandise and identify the list of recipients, heck, let the CFO measure the results, too. You'll teach the CFO a lesson he'll never forget, I'll promise you that!

I did just that, back in 2003. I had a lot of naysayers who thought they knew targeting strategies better than I did.

I created a mini-simulation where employees could contact customers the way they felt was best ... the best outcome was -20% to what my team was doing. I didn't get a lot of negative feedback after that exercise, folks understood what a challenge it was to execute marketing/targeting in a profitable way.

It is time to push back. You are not a ridiculous employee who only wants to have fun with other people's money. You care about return on investment. You care about maintaining "what has always worked". You want to experiment and position your business for future success. You don't want to "spam" people. Prove your worth. Go on the road, and communicate what is known about the customer with your co-workers.

December 28

We are right in the middle of college football "bowl season".

Have you heard about this? For the most part, if you are a college football team that wins at least six games, you're going to be asked to play in a special game, often in a warm climate. Obviously, those who run bowl games, and those who participate in bowl games make money, often lots of money.

But for the college student/athlete participating, the bowl game represents a reward for a year of hard work.

Your year is almost over. What have you done to reward employees for doing a great job? You know as well as I do that you can't just hand out indiscriminate pay raises and promotions, so you have to figure out another way to reward people.

Think carefully about how you reward people for doing a great job.

December 29

As you probably already know, segment customers who purchase merchandise between December 26 and December 31. The motivations of this customer audience are fundamentally different than the motivations of a customer buying on a non-descript day in mid-May.

December 30

If you are a web analyst, make a point to learn a programming language in 2012. Broaden your horizons. Be able to integrate data from different sources, and then analyze customer behavior across all channels, over time.

Your time has come. The mantle of analytics leadership is upon you, given your experience and the data you've analyzed over the past decade. Step up and take on more responsibility!!

December 31

Imagine Dan Fogelberg's "Old Lang Syne" playing in the background, as you wrap-up 2011.

If there is one thing I want for you to take away from our year-long discussion, it is this:
- Learn How To Identify Marketing Slush.

We're so deep in marketing slush that our feet are chilly, we're literally frozen, stuck in our tracks. Our feet are numb.

I simply don't understand when it became acceptable for marketing and analytics experts to shout opinions, opinions that smack of truthiness.

Maybe social media is to blame. Maybe it is just so easy to offer an opinion that now we only offer opinions, opinions not backed by facts. And when people don't listen to us, we just shout our opinions louder, or create sensational subject lines and article titles to encourage people to pay attention to us.

The Groupon discussion always highlights the depth of marketing slush we have to navigate. We don't know if Groupon promotions truly work or not. We don't have the data to know if other companies acquire new customers, or if other companies simply give the farm away to existing customers who were going to purchase anyway. Heck, I'm guilty of the same hype that those who love Groupon are guilty of! I do try, however, to apply facts to my arguments.

Not everybody uses facts.

- "I think that the viral component of a Groupon promotion yields benefits to brands willing to experiment in new channels".

Where is the data to back up this claim?

Few are accountable anymore.

Research organizations make bold predictions about the growth of the mobile channel, or about increases in Christmas sales. When they are wrong (how can their predictions ever be right?), they don't issue a press release outlining how inaccurate their prediction was. No, they dump a bunch of marketing slush on us, and we have to get the shovel out and rescue ourselves from their mess.

And then there's Twitter. My goodness. You should see some of the discussions out there.

- "Motrin alienated Moms, and look what that meant to their social footprint? They're finished."

Are they finished because of a social media mistake? Certainly not. But we boldly predict their demise without any semblance of accountability.

Or you hear this on Twitter.

- "If you're not actively measuring engagement, you will be out of business in three years. #measure"

How does the web analyst know this? You mean to tell me that every single business in America that doesn't measure engagement will be out of business in 2014? Wow.

We need to get our snow shovels out, and we need to dig ourselves out of this endless array of marketing slush.

We need to focus on accountability.

We need to look at customer behavior facts, facts that are measured across time, not facts that are measured in real-time within the confines of a marketing promotion.

We are certainly entitled to an opinion. We need to minimize our habit to state opinions as facts, coupled with bold predictions that we're not held accountable for when we're wrong.

We need to focus on our customer base, doing what is right for our customers.

We need to focus on profit.

You are reading this book because you are a smart marketer, a smart leader, or a smart analytics expert. You know more about your customers than anybody else. Don't let a vendor or a marketing consultant (me included) or a blogger tell you what you have to do.

Do what is right for your customer.

Thank you for taking the time to read this almanac, I appreciate the time you spent with me to get through this text!

www.ingramcontent.com/pod-product-compliance
Lightning Source LLC
Chambersburg PA
CBHW051518170526
45165CB00002B/525